50% OFF TExES Science of Teaching Reading (293) Prep Course!

Dear Customer,

We consider it an honor and a privilege that you chose our TExES Science of Teaching Reading Study Guide. **Included with your purchase is discounted access to the Mometrix TExES 293 Prep Course**. Many TExES 293 courses are needlessly expensive and don't deliver enough value. That is why Test Prep Books has partnered with Mometrix. With their course, you get access to the best TExES Science of Teaching Reading prep material, and **you only pay half price**.

Mometrix has structured their online course to perfectly complement your printed study guide. The TExES 293 Prep Course contains **in-depth lessons** that cover all the most important topics, **50+ video reviews** that explain difficult concepts, over **350 practice questions** to ensure you feel prepared, and more than **300 digital flashcards**, so you can study while you're on the go.

Online TExES Science of Teaching Reading (293) Prep Course

Topics Included:
- Reading Pedagogy
  - Curriculum and Instruction
  - Diverse Learners and Specific Needs
- Reading Development: Foundational Skills
  - Grammar and Comprehension
  - Fluency Acquisition
- Reading Development: Comprehension
  - Vocabulary Development and Word Analysis
  - Context Clues and Affixes

Course Features:
- TExES Science of Teaching Reading Study Guide
  - Get content that complements our best-selling study guide.
- Full-Length Practice Tests
  - With over 350 practice questions, you can test yourself again and again.
- Mobile Friendly
  - If you need to study on the go, the course is easily accessible from your mobile device.
- TExES 293 Flashcards
  - Their course includes a flashcard mode with over 300 content cards to help you study.

To lock in this discounted access, visit mometrix.com/university/texesstr/ or simply scan this QR code with your smartphone. At the checkout page, enter the discount code: **TPBTEXSTR50**

If you have any questions or concerns, please contact Mometrix at support@mometrix.com.

 In Partnership with

Online Resources & Audiobook

Included with your purchase are multiple online resources. This includes the practice tests in an interactive format and this book in audiobook format.

Instructions for accessing these resources can be found on the last page of this book.

TExES Science of Teaching Reading 293 Study Guide

Prep and Practice Test for the STR Exam [2nd Edition]

Lydia Morrison

Copyright © 2025 by TPB Publishing

All rights reserved. No part of this publication may be reproduced, distributed, or transmitted in any form or by any means, including photocopying, recording, or other electronic or mechanical methods, without the prior written permission of the publisher, except in the case of brief quotations embodied in critical reviews and certain other noncommercial uses permitted by copyright law.

Written and edited by TPB Publishing.

TPB Publishing is not associated with or endorsed by any official testing organization. TPB Publishing is a publisher of unofficial educational products. All test and organization names are trademarks of their respective owners. Content in this book is included for utilitarian purposes only and does not constitute an endorsement by TPB Publishing of any particular point of view.

ISBN 13: 9781637758793

Table of Contents

Welcome --- 1

Quick Overview --- 2

Test-Taking Strategies --- 3

Introduction to the TExES Science of Teaching Reading --- 7

Study Prep Plan --- 8

Domain I - Reading Pedagogy --- 13

Foundations of the Science of Teaching Reading --- 13

Foundations of Reading Assessment --- 32

Practice Questions --- 43

Answer Explanations --- 44

Domain II - Reading Development: Foundational Skills --- 45

Oral Language Foundations of Reading Development --- 45

Phonological and Phonemic Awareness --- 54

Print Concepts and Alphabet Knowledge --- 59

Phonics and Other Word Identification Skills --- 66

Syllabication and Morphemic Analysis Skills --- 76

Reading Fluency --- 83

Practice Questions --- 90

Answer Explanations --- 91

Domain III - Reading Development: Comprehension --- 92

Vocabulary Development --- 92

Comprehension Development --- 103

Comprehension of Literary Texts --- 114

Comprehension of Informational Texts ------------------------------ 119

Practice Questions -- 126

Answer Explanations -- 127

Domain IV - Analysis and Response -------------------------- *128*

Analysis and Response -- 128

Practice Questions -- 133

Answer Explanations -- 134

Writing Strategies for Constructed Responses -------------- *135*

Practice Test -- *137*

Reading Pedagogy --- 137

Reading Development: Foundational Skills ---------------------- 139

Reading Development: Comprehension --------------------------- 144

Analysis and Response -- 147

Constructed Response --- 150

Answer Explanations -------------------------------------- *152*

Reading Pedagogy --- 152

Reading Development: Foundational Skills ---------------------- 153

Reading Development: Comprehension --------------------------- 157

Analysis and Response -- 159

Online Resources & Audiobook ------------------------------ *163*

Welcome

Dear Reader,

Welcome to your new Test Prep Books study guide! We are pleased that you chose us to help you prepare for your exam. There are many study options to choose from, and we appreciate you choosing us. Studying can be a daunting task, but we have designed a smart, effective study guide to help prepare you for what lies ahead.

Whether you're a parent helping your child learn and grow, a high school student working hard to get into your dream college, or a nursing student studying for a complex exam, we want to help give you the tools you need to succeed. We hope this study guide gives you the skills and the confidence to thrive, and we can't thank you enough for allowing us to be part of your journey.

In an effort to continue to improve our products, we welcome feedback from our customers. We look forward to hearing from you. Suggestions, success stories, and criticisms can all be communicated by emailing us at support@testprepbooks.com.

Sincerely,

Test Prep Books Team

Quick Overview

As you draw closer to taking your exam, effective preparation becomes more and more important. Thankfully, you have this study guide to help you get ready. Use this guide to help keep your studying on track and refer to it often.

This study guide contains several key sections that will help you be successful on your exam. The guide contains tips for what you should do the night before and the day of the test. Also included are test-taking tips. Knowing the right information is not always enough. Many well-prepared test takers struggle with exams. These tips will help equip you to accurately read, assess, and answer test questions.

A large part of the guide is devoted to showing you what content to expect on the exam and to helping you better understand that content. In this guide are practice test questions so that you can see how well you have grasped the content. Then, answer explanations are provided so that you can understand why you missed certain questions.

Don't try to cram the night before you take your exam. This is not a wise strategy for a few reasons. First, your retention of the information will be low. Your time would be better used by reviewing information you already know rather than trying to learn a lot of new information. Second, you will likely become stressed as you try to gain a large amount of knowledge in a short amount of time. Third, you will be depriving yourself of sleep. So be sure to go to bed at a reasonable time the night before. Being well-rested helps you focus and remain calm.

Be sure to eat a substantial breakfast the morning of the exam. If you are taking the exam in the afternoon, be sure to have a good lunch as well. Being hungry is distracting and can make it difficult to focus. You have hopefully spent lots of time preparing for the exam. Don't let an empty stomach get in the way of success!

When travelling to the testing center, leave earlier than needed. That way, you have a buffer in case you experience any delays. This will help you remain calm and will keep you from missing your appointment time at the testing center.

Be sure to pace yourself during the exam. Don't try to rush through the exam. There is no need to risk performing poorly on the exam just so you can leave the testing center early. Allow yourself to use all of the allotted time if needed.

Remain positive while taking the exam even if you feel like you are performing poorly. Thinking about the content you should have mastered will not help you perform better on the exam.

Once the exam is complete, take some time to relax. Even if you feel that you need to take the exam again, you will be well served by some down time before you begin studying again. It's often easier to convince yourself to study if you know that it will come with a reward!

Test-Taking Strategies

1. Predicting the Answer

When you feel confident in your preparation for a multiple-choice test, try predicting the answer before reading the answer choices. This is especially useful on questions that test objective factual knowledge. By predicting the answer before reading the available choices, you eliminate the possibility that you will be distracted or led astray by an incorrect answer choice. You will feel more confident in your selection if you read the question, predict the answer, and then find your prediction among the answer choices. After using this strategy, be sure to still read all of the answer choices carefully and completely. If you feel unprepared, you should not attempt to predict the answers. This would be a waste of time and an opportunity for your mind to wander in the wrong direction.

2. Reading the Whole Question

Too often, test takers scan a multiple-choice question, recognize a few familiar words, and immediately jump to the answer choices. Test authors are aware of this common impatience, and they will sometimes prey upon it. For instance, a test author might subtly turn the question into a negative, or he or she might redirect the focus of the question right at the end. The only way to avoid falling into these traps is to read the entirety of the question carefully before reading the answer choices.

3. Looking for Wrong Answers

Long and complicated multiple-choice questions can be intimidating. One way to simplify a difficult multiple-choice question is to eliminate all of the answer choices that are clearly wrong. In most sets of answers, there will be at least one selection that can be dismissed right away. If the test is administered on paper, the test taker could draw a line through it to indicate that it may be ignored; otherwise, the test taker will have to perform this operation mentally or on scratch paper. In either case, once the obviously incorrect answers have been eliminated, the remaining choices may be considered. Sometimes identifying the clearly wrong answers will give the test taker some information about the correct answer. For instance, if one of the remaining answer choices is a direct opposite of one of the eliminated answer choices, it may well be the correct answer. The opposite of obviously wrong is obviously right! Of course, this is not always the case. Some answers are obviously incorrect simply because they are irrelevant to the question being asked. Still, identifying and eliminating some incorrect answer choices is a good way to simplify a multiple-choice question.

4. Don't Overanalyze

Anxious test takers often overanalyze questions. When you are nervous, your brain will often run wild, causing you to make associations and discover clues that don't actually exist. If you feel that this may be a problem for you, do whatever you can to slow down during the test. Try taking a deep breath or counting to ten. As you read and consider the question, restrict yourself to the particular words used by the author. Avoid thought tangents about what the author *really* meant, or what he or she was *trying* to say. The only things that matter on a multiple-choice test are the words that are actually in the question. You must avoid reading too much into a multiple-choice question, or supposing that the writer meant

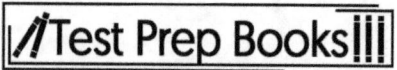

something other than what he or she wrote.

5. No Need for Panic

It is wise to learn as many strategies as possible before taking a multiple-choice test, but it is likely that you will come across a few questions for which you simply don't know the answer. In this situation, avoid panicking. Because most multiple-choice tests include dozens of questions, the relative value of a single wrong answer is small. As much as possible, you should compartmentalize each question on a multiple-choice test. In other words, you should not allow your feelings about one question to affect your success on the others. When you find a question that you either don't understand or don't know how to answer, just take a deep breath and do your best. Read the entire question slowly and carefully. Try rephrasing the question a couple of different ways. Then, read all of the answer choices carefully. After eliminating obviously wrong answers, make a selection and move on to the next question.

6. Confusing Answer Choices

When working on a difficult multiple-choice question, there may be a tendency to focus on the answer choices that are the easiest to understand. Many people, whether consciously or not, gravitate to the answer choices that require the least concentration, knowledge, and memory. This is a mistake. When you come across an answer choice that is confusing, you should give it extra attention. A question might be confusing because you do not know the subject matter to which it refers. If this is the case, don't

eliminate the answer before you have affirmatively settled on another. When you come across an answer choice of this type, set it aside as you look at the remaining choices. If you can confidently assert that one of the other choices is correct, you can leave the confusing answer aside. Otherwise, you will need to take a moment to try to better understand the confusing answer choice. Rephrasing is one way to tease out the sense of a confusing answer choice.

7. Your First Instinct

Many people struggle with multiple-choice tests because they overthink the questions. If you have studied sufficiently for the test, you should be prepared to trust your first instinct once you have carefully and completely read the question and all of the answer choices. There is a great deal of research suggesting that the mind can come to the correct conclusion very quickly once it has obtained all of the relevant information. At times, it may seem to you as if your intuition is working faster even than your reasoning mind. This may in fact be true. The knowledge you obtain while studying may be retrieved from your subconscious before you have a chance to work out the associations that support it. Verify your instinct by working out the reasons that it should be trusted.

8. Key Words

Many test takers struggle with multiple-choice questions because they have poor reading comprehension skills. Quickly reading and understanding a multiple-choice question requires a mixture of skill and experience. To help with this, try jotting down a few key words and phrases on a piece of scrap paper. Doing this concentrates the process of reading and forces the mind to weigh the relative importance of the question's parts. In selecting words and phrases to write down, the test taker thinks about the question more deeply and carefully. This is especially true for multiple-choice questions that are preceded by a long prompt.

9. Subtle Negatives

One of the oldest tricks in the multiple-choice test writer's book is to subtly reverse the meaning of a question with a word like *not* or *except*. If you are not paying attention to each word in the question, you can easily be led astray by this trick. For instance, a common question format is, "Which of the following is...?" Obviously, if the question instead is, "Which of the following is not...?," then the answer will be quite different. Even worse, the test makers are aware of the potential for this mistake and will include one answer choice that would be correct if the question were not negated or reversed. A test taker who misses the reversal will find what he or she believes to be a correct answer and will be so confident that he or she will fail to reread the question and discover the original error. The only way to avoid this is to practice a wide variety of multiple-choice questions and to pay close attention to each and every word.

10. Reading Every Answer Choice

It may seem obvious, but you should always read every one of the answer choices! Too many test takers fall into the habit of scanning the question and assuming that they understand the question because they recognize a few key words. From there, they pick the first answer choice that answers the question they believe they have read. Test takers who read all of the answer choices might discover that one of the latter answer choices is actually *more* correct. Moreover, reading all of the answer choices can remind you of facts related to the question that can help you arrive at the correct answer. Sometimes, a misstatement or incorrect detail in one of the latter answer choices will trigger your memory of the subject and will enable you to find the right answer. Failing to read all of the answer choices is like not reading all of the items on a restaurant menu: you might miss out on the perfect choice.

11. Spot the Hedges

One of the keys to success on multiple-choice tests is paying close attention to every word. This is never truer than with words like *almost*, *most*, *some*, and *sometimes*. These words are called "hedges" because they indicate that a statement is not totally true or not true in every place and time. An absolute statement will contain no hedges, but in many subjects, the answers are not always straightforward or absolute. There are always exceptions to the rules in these subjects. For this reason,

you should favor those multiple-choice questions that contain hedging language. The presence of qualifying words indicates that the author is taking special care with his or her words, which is certainly important when composing the right answer. After all, there are many ways to be wrong, but there is only one way to be right! For this reason, it is wise to avoid answers that are absolute when taking a multiple-choice test. An absolute answer is one that says things are either all one way or all another. They often include words like *every*, *always*, *best*, and *never*. If you are taking a multiple-choice test in a subject that doesn't lend itself to absolute answers, be on your guard if you see any of these words.

12. Long Answers

In many subject areas, the answers are not simple. As already mentioned, the right answer often requires hedges. Another common feature of the answers to a complex or subjective question are qualifying clauses, which are groups of words that subtly modify the meaning of the sentence. If the question or answer choice describes a rule to which there are exceptions or the subject matter is complicated, ambiguous, or confusing, the correct answer will require many words in order to be expressed clearly and accurately. In essence, you should not be deterred by answer choices that seem excessively long. Oftentimes, the author of the text will not be able to write the correct answer without offering some qualifications and modifications. Your job is to read the answer choices thoroughly and completely and to select the one that most accurately and precisely answers the question.

13. Restating to Understand

Sometimes, a question on a multiple-choice test is difficult not because of what it asks but because of how it is written. If this is the case, restate the question or answer choice in different words. This process serves a couple of important purposes. First, it forces you to concentrate on the core of the question. In order to rephrase the question accurately, you have to understand it well. Rephrasing the question will concentrate your mind on the key words and ideas. Second, it will present the information to your mind in a fresh way. This process may trigger your memory and render some useful scrap of information picked up while studying.

14. True Statements

Sometimes an answer choice will be true in itself, but it does not answer the question. This is one of the main reasons why it is essential to read the question carefully and completely before proceeding to the answer choices. Too often, test takers skip ahead to the answer choices and look for true statements. Having found one of these, they are content to select it without reference to the question above. The savvy test taker will always read the entire question before turning to the answer choices. Then, having settled on a correct answer choice, he or she will refer to the original question and ensure that the selected answer is relevant. The mistake of choosing a correct-but-irrelevant answer choice is especially common on questions related to specific pieces of objective knowledge.

15. No Patterns

One of the more dangerous ideas that circulates about multiple-choice tests is that the correct answers tend to fall into patterns. These erroneous ideas range from a belief that B and C are the most common right answers, to the idea that an unprepared test-taker should answer "A-B-A-C-A-D-A-B-A." It cannot be emphasized enough that pattern-seeking of this type is exactly the WRONG way to approach a multiple-choice test. To begin with, it is highly unlikely that the test maker will plot the correct answers according to some predetermined pattern. The questions are scrambled and delivered in a random order. Furthermore, even if the test maker was following a pattern in the assignation of correct answers, there is no reason why the test taker would know which pattern he or she was using. Any attempt to discern a pattern in the answer choices is a waste of time and a distraction from the real work of taking the test. A test taker would be much better served by extra preparation before the test than by reliance on a pattern in the answers.

Introduction to the TExES Science of Teaching Reading

Function of the Test

As of January 1, 2021, the state of Texas requires teacher candidates pursuing an intern, probationary, or standard certificate in specific fields to establish their proficiency in the science of teaching reading. Teachers who already possess standard certification do not need to meet this proficiency requirement unless they choose to add one of the specified fields to their current certification. The affected certificate fields include the following: Core Subjects with Science of Teaching Reading (Early Childhood and Grades 4-8), English Language Arts and Reading (and Reading/Social Studies) with Science of Teaching Reading (Grades 4-8), and Early Childhood (Prekindergarten-Grade 3).

Test Administration

The TExES Science of Teaching Reading examination is offered year-round at testing centers in Texas and at other various locations around the United States. You can find testing centers and appointment availabilities at www.tx.nesinc.com/TestView.aspx?f=HTML_FRAG/TX293_TestPage.html. It costs $136 to take the exam.

If a test taker does not receive a passing score, he or she may register for a retake, which can be taken no earlier than 30 days after the previous attempt. Registration for a retake will not be available until the previous attempt's scores are posted.

Test Format

This test is a computer-administrated test (CAT). Test takers have a five hour timeframe within which to complete the test; 15 minutes are allotted at the beginning for CAT orientation, and the remaining 4 hours and 45 minutes are designated for completing the exam. There are 90 multiple-choice questions and one constructed-response question. The test does not need to be completed in a specific order.

The STR exam includes questions with video and audio elements, so testing centers will provide headsets for use during the exam. Test takers may not bring any outside materials with them.

Scoring

During the eight month introductory period of the exam, test takers will receive a pass or fail score based on a preliminary threshold. This threshold will be reassessed after the introductory period and the agreed upon passing score will be implemented on September 6th, 2021.

Scoring is determined by the test in its entirety; individual sections do not receive their own scores. Thus, a failing score necessitates a retake of the whole test. Final scores are scheduled to be released within 28 days of the exam date.

The selected-response questions are objective and scored automatically. The constructed response question will be read and scored by two individuals. If there is no consensus regarding the score, then additional scorers will be consulted.

Study Prep Plan

1 **Schedule** - Use one of our study schedules below or come up with one of your own.

2 **Relax** - Test anxiety can hurt even the best students. There are many ways to reduce stress. Find the one that works best for you.

3 **Execute** - Once you have a good plan in place, be sure to stick to it.

One Week Study Schedule

Day 1	Domain I - Reading Pedagogy
Day 2	Foundations of Reading Assessment
Day 3	Domain II - Reading Development: Foundational Skills
Day 4	Phonics and Other Word Identification Skills
Day 5	Domain III - Reading Development: Comprehension
Day 6	Comprehension of Literary Texts

Two Week Study Schedule

Day 1	Domain I - Reading Pedagogy	Day 8	Reading Fluency
Day 2	Strategies for Encouraging the...	Day 9	Domain III - Reading Development...
Day 3	Foundations of Reading Assessment	Day 10	Comprehension Development
Day 4	Domain II - Reading Development...	Day 11	Comprehension of Literary Texts
Day 5	Phonological and Phonemic Awareness	Day 12	Comprehension of Informational Texts
Day 6	Phonics and Other Word Identification Skills	Day 13	Practice Test
Day 7	Syllabication and Morphemic Analysis...	Day 14	Take Your Exam!

Study Prep Plan

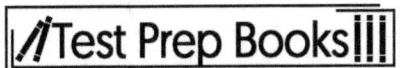

One Month Study Schedule

Day 1	Domain I - Reading Pedagogy	Day 11	Print Concepts and Alphabet Knowledge	Day 21	Comprehension Development
Day 2	Decoding, Encoding, and the Stages of...	Day 12	Assessing Print Awareness...	Day 22	Metacognition and Critical Thinking Skills
Day 3	Strategies for Encouraging the...	Day 13	Phonics and Other Word Identification...	Day 23	Comprehension of Literary Texts
Day 4	Tiered Instructional Models	Day 14	Sight Word Instruction	Day 24	Comprehension of Informational Texts
Day 5	Foundations of Reading Assessment	Day 15	Self-Monitoring and Pre-Teaching Strategies	Day 25	Practice Questions
Day 6	Group and Individual Classroom Reading...	Day 16	Syllabication and Morphemic...	Day 26	Domain IV - Analysis and Response
Day 7	Practice Questions	Day 17	Reading Fluency	Day 27	Practice Questions
Day 8	Domain II - Reading Development...	Day 18	Practice Questions	Day 28	Practice Test
Day 9	Standard American English and Its Deviations	Day 19	Domain III - Reading Development: Comprehension	Day 29	Answer Explanations
Day 10	Phonological and Phonemic Awareness	Day 20	Independent Word-Learning Strategies	Day 30	Take Your Exam!

As you study for your test, we'd like to take the opportunity to remind you that you are capable of great things! With the right tools and dedication, you truly can do anything you set your mind to. The fact that you are holding this book right now shows how committed you are. In case no one has told you lately, you've got this! Our intention behind including this coloring page is to give you the chance to take some time to engage your creative side when you need a little brain-break from studying. As a company, we want to encourage people like you to achieve their dreams by providing good quality study materials for the tests and certifications that improve careers and change lives. As individuals, many of us have taken such tests in our careers, and we know how challenging this process can be. While we can't come alongside you and cheer you on personally, we can offer you the space to recall your purpose, reconnect with your passion, and refresh your brain through an artistic practice. We wish you every success, and happy studying!

Domain I - Reading Pedagogy

Foundations of the Science of Teaching Reading

Research and Reliable Sources

While teachers have access to an ever-increasing volume of sources, not every source is reliable. Some research is biased and presents facts that are not necessarily true; other sources are not researched at all and are based purely on personal experience. Teachers need to evaluate their sources for credibility before using them in the classroom, particularly when using material from the internet.

Here are some helpful questions you can ask yourself to determine whether a source is credible.

- Is the source published by a reputable organization? If you are not sure, research the publisher and make sure that it is trustworthy. Some examples of reputable sources are research journals, academic presses, and well-known organizations (such as libraries or museums). If you are conducting research online, you will find that these sources typically have web addresses that end with .edu or .gov. Some research journals are especially reliable because they have been **peer reviewed**, which means that they have been vetted by a team of experts before publication. Unreliable sources include personal blogs and social media posts; online, these sources will usually be on websites ending with .com.

- Who is the author, and what are their credentials? The most reliable information comes from experienced researchers and professionals. Information about personal experience, such as a post on a teaching blog, may help teachers brainstorm new ideas, but it is not as reliable as source material for research.

- Does the source use evidence to back its claims? Good research is grounded in fact, not speculation.

- What is the date of the source? Research is always advancing, so older sources are typically not as reliable as newer ones.

- Is the source's writing of a high quality? Numerous grammatical mistakes, typos, and other errors indicate that the author or organization is not credible.

- Is the source unbiased? This question is particularly important when evaluating the findings from studies. For example, consider a study on the risks and benefits of teaching reading with computers and tablets. If this study is conducted by a major electronics company, it is not unbiased: the researchers have a considerable stake in the findings, and they may design a study that favors computer use.

Important Reading Guidelines and Standards

Texas Prekindergarten Guidelines

The Texas Prekindergarten Guidelines were established by the Texas Education Agency (TEA). These guidelines, which were last revised in 2015, provide training for teachers to understand the different learning development stages children go through prior to entering prekindergarten (pre-K). The guidelines go hand in hand with the Texas Essential Knowledge and Skills (TEKS).

Early development, language skills, family life, and special needs and disabilities are among the factors that affect a child's ability to learn in a class environment. The Texas Prekindergarten Guidelines take all of these factors into consideration before providing instructional advice to educators. Not only will these guidelines help pre-K teachers, but they will also inform those who teach kindergarten through grade 6. This essential information will be especially helpful to reading teachers.

TEKS for English Language Arts and Reading

The TEKS are state-mandated standards for student learning. These standards establish what public school children's curriculum should contain in a variety of subjects. The requirements for student reading levels fall under English Language Arts and Reading (ELAR). TEKS require that all curricula must encompass the "**seven strands of knowledge**." These include inquiry, research, author's intent, comprehension, recognition of different genres, language skills, and types of response. Teachers of students in kindergarten through grade 6 are able to meet ELAR requirements in a variety of ways, such as speaking exercises, vocabulary quizzes, reading and writing assignments, and more.

TEKS and ELAR encourage teachers to provide assignments of varying difficulty. This will alert them to their students' strengths and areas where they will need further assistance. Considering the needs of children with disabilities and those who speak English as a second language and implementing ways to instruct these students is also required. To learn more about ELAR, you can visit the TEA's website at tea.texas.gov.

Classroom Activities That Integrate Language Skills

Role play is an entertaining and low-stress way for students to practice speaking. Students playing store can practice vocabulary. Students acting out a book that the class has just read can practice summarizing a text. Role play can take place with the class as a whole or in small groups.

Literature circles are groups of students who read the same text independently and meet to discuss it. The teacher groups students based on reading level or common interests and allows them to choose an appropriate book. The teacher may also assign each student a different role, such as leading discussion or collecting new vocabulary words. This task delegation can help keep the group on track and teach leadership skills. Literature circles foster social connection and critical thinking skills, but they are not suitable for very young students.

Discussion circles are similar to literature circles, but they focus on discussing topics, issues, or ideas rather than the text itself. In an ESL classroom or lower grade, teachers may guide students to discuss a general topic rather than a text. For example, if the theme of the book is overcoming obstacles, students might reflect on obstacles they have encountered in their own lives and discuss their experiences. For students with more advanced language skills, discussion circles are a place to practice persuasive skills and debate more abstract topics such as moral and ethical principles.

In **jigsaw discussions**, the teacher assigns each student or small group a different reading. After everyone has read their assignment, the students meet and present their findings to the group. For example, students might each read about a different country in South America before reconvening to give mini presentations and combine their information into a travel guide. By summarizing material in front of a group, students practice comprehension, speaking, and critical thinking skills. Jigsaw discussions also help students learn to collaborate effectively and can encourage notetaking.

Language games help students practice their language skills while providing a break from more serious class activities. Games can involve anything from Simon Says to reading a word and then drawing it for the other students to guess.

Stages of Reading Development

Reading is one of the most important abilities humans have developed. Although some children begin reading before entering school, the majority are officially taught to read in the first grade. From novices to voracious readers, everyone started somewhere. It is important for reading teachers to understand that there are five specific reading development stages. The following provides descriptions of these five stages and the characteristics students display in each stage.

Emergent
The **emergent** stage of reading development is the pre-reading or pre-alphabetic stage when children develop their fine motor skills. Children between the ages of 6 months and 6 years, including those in pre-K and kindergarten, are considered emerging readers. Before they learn to read, children learn to observe. They recognize when people speak to them and are able to identify different sounds. They also get acquainted with different images and objects. Reading to children up to 6 years old familiarizes them with the look and feel of books as well as the tones used to read stories. A small child may touch or point to pictures and words in books; if the same book is read more than once, the child may recognize the characters and learn to recognize when the storylines change. At this point, children are ready to learn the alphabet and recite parts of stories. They may also start writing specific words, drawing pictures, or reenacting scenes from stories with their toys.

Beginning
Children in the **beginning** stage are usually 6 or 7 years old and entering kindergarten, first grade, or second grade. They know part or all of the alphabet, which prepares them to start reading and decoding. On average, children in this stage can read up to six hundred words. This is achieved by teaching them how to sound out words and say them phonetically. They should learn the relationship between the words they are reading and their meanings (**decoding**). Teachers can have their students read passages of words out loud in class or individually to ensure they have learned how to pronounce them. They can then ask the children questions about what they have just read, such as the following: *What is happening in this part of the story? How do you think the character feels? What does [insert word] mean?*

Transitional
Children in the **transitional** stage (also known as the *confirmation and fluency stage*) are able to read. They can now be challenged by more advanced material. Instructors can begin giving these children vocabulary and spelling tests, teaching them the basics of grammar, and questioning them about what specific sentences mean. These students are typically between the ages of 7 and 9, and they are in second, third, or fourth grade.

Intermediate
By age 9, reading should be a regular part of a child's education. They will be reading in almost every class. The **intermediate** stage includes children aged 9 to 15 in grades 3 through 10. These students

Domain I - Reading Pedagogy

should be able to engage in more advanced discussions about different types reading material, including novels, textbooks, magazines, and news articles. Their decoding skills will be much sharper than in previous stages, and their vocabulary should be much improved. Teachers should note how well these children learn in relation to reading; students may be auditory, kinesthetic, or visual learners.

Advanced

The **advanced** reading stage includes anyone aged 15 and older, but younger readers may also be included in this category. At this point, children and adults should be able to form multiple viewpoints when reading. They not only read to be educated, but they also read for pleasure and personal knowledge. They will be able to read and comprehend documents of varying difficulty. Advanced readers also understand that what they read can influence their views and opinions, so they are much more selective.

Decoding, Encoding, and the Stages of Spelling Development

Decoding and encoding are reciprocal phonological skills, meaning that their steps are opposite of each other.

Decoding

Decoding is the application of letter-sound correspondences, letter patterns, and other phonics relationships that help students read and correctly pronounce words. Decoding helps students to recognize and read words quickly, increasing reading fluency and comprehension. The steps of the decoding process are as follows:

1. The student identifies a written letter or letter combination.
2. The student identifies the sound of that letter or letter combination.
3. The student understands how the word's different letters or letter combinations fit together.
4. The student verbally blends the letter and letter combinations together to form a word.

Blending Consonant and Vowel Sounds to Decode Single-Syllable Words

The ability to break apart a word into its individual phonemes is referred to as **segmenting**. Segmenting words can greatly aid in a child's ability to recognize, read, and spell an entire word. In literacy instruction, **blending** is when the reader connects segmented parts to create an entire word. Segmenting and blending practice work together like pieces of a puzzle to help children practice newly acquired vocabulary. Educators can approach segmenting and blending using a multi-sensory approach. For example, a child can manipulate letter blocks to build words and pull them apart. An educator may even ask the child to listen to the word being said and ask him or her to find the letter blocks that build each phoneme, one at a time:

/m/ /u/ /g/

/b/ /a/ /t/

/r/ /u/ /n/

Once children are able to blend and segment phonemes, they are ready for the more complex skill of blending and segmenting syllables, onsets, and rimes. Using the same multi-sensory approach, children may practice blending the syllables of familiar words on a word wall, using letter blocks, paper and pencil, or sounding them out loud. Once they blend the words together, students can then practice segmenting those same words, studying their individual syllables, letters, and sounds. Educators may again read a word out loud and ask children to write or build the first syllable, followed by the next, and so on. The very same practice can be used to identify the onset. Children can work on writing and/or building this sound followed by the word's rime. Word families and rhyming words are ideal for this type of exercise so that children can more readily see the parts of each word.

Once children have demonstrated the ability to independently blend and segment phonemes, syllables, onsets, and rimes, educators may present a more challenging exercise that involves substitutions and deletions. As these are more complex skills, children will likely benefit from repeated practice and modeling. Using word families and words that rhyme when teaching this skill will make the activity more enjoyable, and it will also greatly aid in a child's overall comprehension.

Substitution and Deletion Using Onset and Rime				
Word	Onset Deletion	Rime Deletion	Onset Substitution	Rime Substitution
Run	un	r	Fun	rat
Bun	un	b	Gun	bat
Sun	un	s	Nun	sat

Substitution and Deletion Using Phonemes		
Word	Phoneme substitution	Phoneme Deletion
Sit	sat	si
Bit	bat	bi
Hit	hat	hi

Substitution and Deletion Using Syllables		
Word	Syllable Substitution	Syllable Deletion
cement	lament or, cedar	ce
moment	statement, or motive	mo
basement	movement, or baseball	base

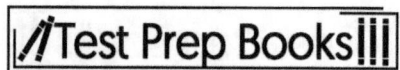

Encoding

Encoding is the spelling of words. In order to properly spell words, students must be familiar with letter/sound correspondences. Students must be able to put together phonemes, digraphs or blends, morphological units, consonant/vowel patterns, etc. The steps of encoding are identified below:

1. The student understands that letters and sounds make up words.
2. The student segments the sound parts of a word.
3. The student identifies the letter or letter combinations that correspond to each sound part.
4. The student writes the letters and letter combinations in order to create the word.

Because the stages of decoding and encoding are reciprocal skills, phonics knowledge supports the development of reading and spelling. Likewise, the development of spelling skills reinforces phonics and decoding. In fact, the foundation of all good spelling programs is alignment with reading instruction and students' reading levels.

The Stages of Spelling Development

Phonics instruction begins with simple syllable patterns and then progresses toward more complex patterns, the sounds of morphemes, and strategies for decoding multisyllabic words. Through this process, new vocabulary is developed. Sight word instruction should not begin until students are able to decode target words with automaticity and accuracy. Spelling is the last instructional component to be introduced.

Spelling development begins with the **pre-phonetic stage**, which is marked by an incomplete understanding of the alphabetic principle and letter-sound correspondences. During this stage, students participate in **precommunicative writing**, which appears to be a jumble of letter-like forms rather than a series of discrete letters. Students' precommunicative writing samples can be used as informal

Domain I - Reading Pedagogy

assessments of their understanding of the alphabetic principle and knowledge of letter-sound correspondences.

Pre-phonetic stage of spelling development

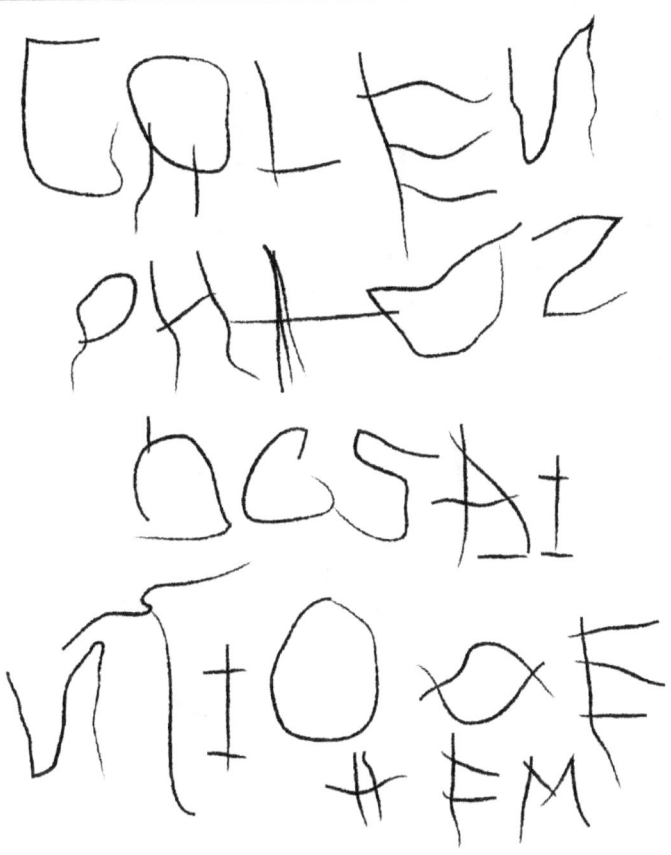

The pre-phonetic stage is followed by the **semiphonetic stage**, in which students understand that letters represent sounds. The alphabetic principle may be understood, but letter recognition may not yet be fully developed. In this stage, single letters may be used to represent entire words (e.g., *U* for *you*). Other times, multiple syllables within words may be omitted. Writing produced by students in this stage is still virtually unreadable. Teachers may ask students to provide drawings to supplement their writing to better determine what a student intended to write.

The third stage in spelling development is the **phonetic stage**. In this stage, students have mastered letter-sound correspondences. Although letters may be written backward or upside down, phonetic spellers are able to write all of the letters in the alphabet. Because phonetic spellers have limited sight vocabulary, they will often spell irregular words incorrectly; however, these incorrectly spelled words may phonetically sound like the spoken word. Additionally, student writing becomes systematic. For example, students are likely to use one letter to represent a digraph or letter blend (e.g., *f* for /ph/).

Domain I - Reading Pedagogy

Spelling instruction of common consonant patterns, short vowel sounds, and common affixes or rimes can begin during the phonetic stage.

Phonetic stage of writing

Word walls are advantageous during the phonetic stage because they provide visual groupings of words that share common consonant-vowel patterns or letter clusters. Students are encouraged to add words to each group. As a result, word walls promote strategic spelling, vocabulary development, common letter combinations, and common morphological units.

The **transitional stage** of spelling occurs when a student has developed a small sight vocabulary and a solid understanding of letter-sound correspondences. Thus, spelling dependence on phonology decreases. Instead, dependence on visual representation and word structure increases. As sight word vocabulary increases during the transitional stage, the correct spelling of irregular words will also increase. However, students may still struggle to spell words with long vowel sounds.

Transitional stage of spelling

Differentiation of spelling instruction often begins during the transitional stage. Instruction ought to be guided by data collected through informal observations and assessments. Depending on individual needs, lessons may include sight word recognition, morphology, etymology, reading, and writing. Students can begin learning about homophones during the transitional stage. **Homophones** are words that sound the same but have different spellings and meanings (e.g., *their* and *there*). Additionally, students should be expected to begin writing full sentences. Writing reinforces phonics, vocabulary, and correct spelling of words.

The **conventional stage** comes last, occurring after a student's sight word vocabulary is well developed and the student is able to read fluently with comprehension. By this stage, students know the basic rules of phonics. They are able to deal with consonants, multiple vowel-consonant blends, homophones, digraphs, and irregular spellings. Due to an increase in sight word recognition at this stage, a conventional speller is able to recognize when a word is spelled incorrectly.

It is at the conventional stage that spelling instruction can begin to focus on content-specific vocabulary words and words with unusual spellings. In order to further reinforce vocabulary development of such content-specific words and apply phonic skills, students should be encouraged to use the correct spelling of such words within various writing activities.

For even the best conventional spellers, some words will still cause consistent trouble. Students can keep track of words that they consistently spell incorrectly or find confusing in word banks so they can isolate and eventually eliminate their individualized errors. Students can use their word banks as references when they come across a word with which they struggle. Students may also spend time consciously committing the words in their banks to memory through verbal or written practice.

Components of Reading

There are five components of reading: **phonics** (connecting word sounds to written language), **phonemic awareness** (identifying phonemes, sounds, and syllables), **vocabulary**, **fluency**, and **reading comprehension**. Reading comprehension, defined as the ability to understand what is being read, also has five dimensions: **listening comprehension**, **vocabulary development**, **literary analysis**, **analysis of informational text**, and **responses to text**. Whether a child is reading out loud to a class, being read to, or reading by themselves, it is the teacher's job to make sure they know what the words actually mean.

A child's ability to listen is one of the first things parents and teachers test when teaching them to read. Learning to listen well is a skill everyone needs. Studies have shown that people who do not listen well typically are not great readers. According to listenwise.com, a measly 36 percent of fourth graders read efficiently, and a lack of listening comprehension plays a part in that.

Listening skills also impact vocabulary development. Children develop their vocabularies both directly (teacher instruction) and indirectly (overheard conversations, talking, and reading). The more they read and engage with others, the more extensive their vocabularies will be.

By grade 6, children will begin working on their literary analysis skills. Not only will they need to be able to comprehend what they read on a surface level, but they will be expected to ascertain the big picture and meaning of the texts they read. At this point, children will have read textbooks, short stories, poetry, and novels. They will be asked to prepare book reports and participate in open discussions about the books they have read, which will help the teacher determine the level of their fluency and reading comprehension skills.

Instructors can help students develop their analysis skills by asking specific questions about the text: what happened in the plot, what the conflict was, who the main characters were, from whose point of view the story was told, how it made them feel, and if they think there is a **moral**, or lesson, to be gained from the story. As students are initially guided through the analysis process, they will eventually learn how to do it on their own as their skills develop.

Strategies for Encouraging the Enjoyment of Reading

Teaching students *how* to read is one thing; training them to *enjoy* reading is another. Below are some strategies for encouraging reading in the classroom:

1. Model the attitude toward reading that you would like to see in your students. Attitude is contagious; if you show your students that you enjoy reading, they will learn to be enthusiastic about it as well.

2. Create activities that allow students to choose which book they will read. Selecting their own books gives students a sense of agency, which in turn makes them more engaged in their reading.

3. Recommend books to individual students. If a student mentions a topic or genre that interests them, recommend a book related to that interest. When teaching on a subject, offer suggested reading alongside the assigned reading for students who are interested in the topic and want to learn more.

4. Do not allow students to struggle too much on their own. If reading becomes an immensely frustrating experience, students will avoid it. You can prevent this problem by selecting appropriately complex material for your students and giving struggling readers extra help.

5. Create a class environment where reading is a positive activity. Do not call students negative names like "nerd" when they read; discourage other students from using those terms as well. Praising students for reading is also helpful.

6. Read aloud to your students and encourage parents to do the same. Listening enables students to enjoy literature that is above their reading level. Reading aloud is particularly important for young

students who cannot yet read interesting material by themselves, and it promotes a positive attitude toward reading in students of all ages.

7. Encourage students to read at home, not just at school. Reading challenges can be useful, particularly over school breaks.

Implementing Developmentally Appropriate Instruction

The following are key factors to consider when planning reading instruction:

1. Assess knowledge and skills in the specific area(s) of reading.

2. Identify the prerequisite skills that are required for students to benefit from instruction.

3. Properly pace the instruction of such skills.

4. Understand the complexity of the skills and content that should be presented.

5. Provide scaffolding to ensure that all students can access higher-level reading knowledge and skills.

Teachers can evaluate student advancement more effectively with smaller group sizes. Therefore, initial assessments should be used to differentiate instruction and to group students according to their abilities and skill levels. Students who have mastered the skill(s) can move on to more complex tasks at a faster pace while working at their seats independently. This gives the instructor time to meet with students who need more remediation and teacher direction. Students who need the most help should meet with the teacher individually for scaffolded remediation of less complex tasks. Struggling students also benefit from slower-paced lessons and additional practice.

Factors That Can Affect Students' Reading Development

Teachers must remember that a number of factors affect students' reading development. In today's ever-online world, many children spend more time on electronic devices than they do reading books. This can present a challenge to educators when it comes to engaging students in the classroom.

Daily Engagement
Although students spend hours working on their reading skills at school, they do not necessarily exert much effort at home. On average, educators recommend that children spend up to 30 minutes per day reading outside the classroom. The students' stage of development can affect this; the number of words children can read in 30 minutes depends on their reading level. This can cause frustration for both children and their caregivers, and they may forgo reading at home altogether.

Screen Time
Once children have left school for the day, there is no guarantee that they are going to practice reading at home. Instead, they may be spending time on their electronic devices. Studies have shown that children who spend one hour or more online have lower literacy skills than those who don't.

Difficulties with Curriculum
When teaching reading, it is crucial to employ a variety of methods and to consider the needs of each child. When teaching phonics, the use of visuals, sight word exercises, and writing exercises can help

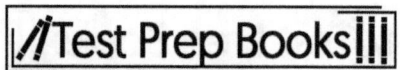

improve students' skills. Another helpful strategy is **structural analysis**, in which students learn word parts such as prefixes and suffixes; to implement this strategy in an engaging way, you can use games and call-and-response exercises to teach children the different prefixes and suffixes. You might also consider breaking students into small groups when they work on exercises.

Children coming from various cultural backgrounds may have different approaches to learning to read. For example, some languages are read right to left rather than the American standard of left to right. A child's socioeconomic background may also affect how well he or she learns to read. For instance, students coming from lower-income families are less likely to attend daycare or pre-K—two places where children typically learn early language skills.

Student-Centered Learning

Teachers should strive to further **student-centered learning** (also known as **learner-centered education**), which refers to educational practices that allow students to make choices about how or what they will learn. For example, a teacher who allows students to write essays on subjects that interest them instead of assigning a topic is practicing student-centered learning. Teachers who use this approach may also allow students to be involved in choosing the details of what they learn (such as which book the class will read) and the methods by which they will be assessed (such as whether they will be assigned a test, a presentation, or an essay). Here are some instructional methods that further this approach:

Ask guiding questions instead of providing answers. Asking questions motivates students to be curious and explore the material for themselves instead of just memorizing facts. For example, a teacher who begins a lesson by listing out characteristics of poetry is only stating facts, while a teacher who asks students to think of factors that differentiate poetry and prose is engaging their critical thinking skills and teaching them to think independently.

Break students into small groups for discussion or activities. For example, a teacher might divide students into groups and have each discuss a different aspect of a novel. After these discussions, each group would give a short presentation to the rest of the class and explain their thoughts.

Give students options, both in learning and evaluation. For example, a teacher could allow students to guide their own learning by giving them time for independent reading. In a similar way, a teacher could let students choose whether they want to give a presentation or create a poster: this choice would allow students to select a format that interests them and caters to their strengths.

Information-Rich Environment

Teachers should work to build **information-rich classrooms**, meaning that it is easy for students to access information in a variety of ways. A classroom that has few books or independent learning activities is not information-rich. Instead, it should include a variety of books that appeal to students with different interests as well as activities designed to engage students. There are countless ways to make your classroom more information-rich; below are some ideas to get you started.

Build a rich classroom library. There should be plenty of books featuring a variety of topics that can engage students with different interests. Classroom libraries are also a great place to include multicultural and diverse literature, as doing so will help minority students feel included and spark others' interest in learning about new cultures.

Integrate technology into your classroom. Computers and tablets can help students who have high technological literacy but are not interested in reading engage with the material. For example, a student who plays video games at home but thinks reading is nerdy may be more motivated to read on a device. Technology can also make your material more accessible to children with special needs, as many children who are on the autism spectrum or have other conditions feel overstimulated by in-person contact and prefer to interact with devices.

Use your wall space. Empty walls create an unwelcoming environment that is not conducive to learning. Walls are an excellent space to create collaborative posters about the material your students are learning, put up charts that will help your students learn new information, and display student work.

Differentiating Classroom Instruction

The following are ways for educators to organize and manage differentiated reading instruction and interventions to meet the needs of all students:

1. Use flexible grouping, individualized instruction, and whole-class instruction as needed.

2. Use all components of their state's adopted materials to make grade-level content accessible for all students.

3. Create intervention groups according to the severity of student needs.

Reading instruction begins with daily whole-class lessons that are conducted to introduce new skills. The remaining time of a reading lesson should be dedicated to independent practice for those who have mastered the skill and intervention time for students who are progressing towards the skill.

Lessons should utilize materials adopted by the practitioner's own state. These materials have been evaluated for consistency with the state's standards and benchmarks. Materials that have been evaluated by one's own state include textbooks, technology-based resources, curriculum sets, and tests. Thus, there are enough materials to use with all types of learners to ensure accessibility for all students.

Students should be assessed during daily lessons. Formative assessments can be done on a daily basis through informal observations. Summative assessments can be done weekly. The teacher ought to use student performance on such assessments to organize the students into smaller intervention groups. The organization of such groups helps to ensure that all students are provided with differentiated interventions on the exact skills in which they struggle. Students who display difficulty in a skill should meet with a teacher for one-on-one or small-group remediation more frequently than students who have mastered the skill. These latter students will be given more independent work at their seats. Groups can be changed accordingly as students' performance changes.

Another way to differentiate instruction is through groups and collaboration when learning or reviewing reading material. In class, there are two forms of grouping instruction: teacher-based and student-based. A well-balanced and flexible learning environment will incorporate both types of grouping exercises to help students approach reading from multiple angles and practice problem-solving and critical-thinking skills. Students also strengthen social skills through flexible grouping.

Teacher-based grouping is organized by the instructor. This is the best method for introducing students to new material and exploring key concepts. Instructors may also choose to break the class up into small groups to provide instruction and work with students individually while the class is working. The goal

here is to monitor students directly and provide differentiated instruction when necessary. This is the more variable of the two groupings and provides a more direct line for teacher intervention. However, students can also grasp concepts by interacting with their peers.

Student-based grouping focuses on students dictating the way the group is formed, essentially freeing the teacher to observe how they are interacting with others and approaching reading topics. This can be done by giving students the option to form their groups independently or by simply conducting a class discussion, which allows students to talk about the reading amongst themselves as opposed to merely listening to a lecture by the instructor. Posing questions for the class is a great way for students to learn correct answers and ask questions through simple conversation. Student-based groups are also excellent for school projects, allowing group members to pool their knowledge for success.

Flexible grouping relies on utilizing both teacher-based and student-based groupings throughout the instructional period. Using one more than the other is not necessarily unbalanced, but the instructor should try to incorporate both groupings in order to broaden the students' experiences. The teacher's choice in using either method should also relate to how they are implementing differentiated teaching methods. Educators can combine the use of grouping to suit activities and lessons for all areas in which students may be facing difficulties in order to boost confidence and clarify material.

Tiered Instructional Models

Response to Intervention Process (RTI) is a process designed to help struggling students catch up through intervention and monitoring in a general education classroom. Students who suffer from undiagnosed reading disorders, attention issues, or even ELL students struggling to learn the language may begin to fall behind the rest of the students in reading skills. RTI is an informal intervention process done by the school that focuses on utilizing research and technology to help the student "catch up" to the rest of the class. The school's RTI teams will review assessments taken of each child in the classroom to determine which students need these instructional interventions. Teachers track students through **progress monitoring**, a process that measures whether or not the interventions are making a difference.

Although there are various ways to do RTI, it is usually set up as a three-tier system of support, also known as **multi-tier system of supports (MTSS)**. The tiers below are in order from least to most intense.

Tier 1: High-Quality Classroom Instruction, Screening, and Group Interventions

In **Tier 1 interventions**, the entire classroom is assessed using universal screening, where everyone's skillset is measured in a general education classroom using methods that have been proven to be effective. Students who receive Tier 1 support are generally divided into small groups based on their skill level. Many students receive Tier 1 support because their math or reading skills are not quite at grade level. Progress of Tier 1 instruction is monitored, and many students are able to effectively catch up to grade level.

Tier 2: Targeted Interventions

Tier 2 interventions are targeted interventions that take place outside of regular classroom time and give more detailed attention to the struggling student. These may be conducted during extracurricular activities or electives.

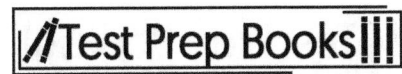

Tier 3: Intensive Interventions and Comprehensive Evaluation

Tier 3 interventions are intensive interventions often done one-on-one or in small groups with other special-needs children. Usually only one or two students in a classroom will need this kind of instruction, so one-on-one help is more readily available for this tier.

Oral Fluency Assessments

Being able to effectively evaluate student performance enables teachers to develop the best instructions to help their students reach their potential. Reading assessments are key to identifying individual strengths and weaknesses, so both formal and informal assessments should be used in the classroom. Being able to successfully gauge individual reading levels means looking at essential performance indicators of rate and accuracy.

An **oral fluency assessment** should be used to see how students approach reading as a whole. This assessment uses a text at or slightly below the students' reading level to examine the number of words they can read within one minute. Based on how many correct words the students read, an instructor can determine how advanced they are in developing reading skills. The number of times students incorrectly read words and the length of time it takes for them to read the text will also determine their level of fluency. Fluency assessments also consider the way in which students read (e.g., whether the language flows or is stalled).

There are four levels of fluency. Levels 1 and 2 reflect nonfluency; these students will need more instruction to hone their reading skills, which may entail various kinds of differentiated instruction. Level 1 is the lowest; these students read word by word and lack tone in their reading. Levels 3 and 4 represent fluent readership. Level 4 reflects the students' ability to read phrases consistently and accurately without having to repeat words.

When considering the results of such assessments, it is important for instructors to note where students struggled in the reading and to analyze why the reading issues exist. Did certain words confuse the student, or did the student just seem unsure of their own abilities? Did certain grammatical phrasing confuse the reader? Asking questions like these will help find root problems and enable the specialist to construct actionable plans to steer improvement. Since such issues can indicate a diverse literacy profile, early identification is very important. These assessments should also be used to track student progress and assess how effective instruction is in overcoming core issues.

Dyslexia and Dysgraphia

When a student displays intense or specific difficulties with reading material, it may be indicative of a learning disability. It is important for educators to understand that learning disabilities are relatively common and can be overcome. To help students do this, however, an instructor must be mindful of the types and effects of various learning disorders. Addressing these learning disabilities is crucial for early development.

Reading disorders are when students exhibit difficulties reading or understanding the written word. One of the most common reading disorders is **dyslexia**. A common sign of dyslexia is that the student will reverse the order of letters and thus confuse sounds or misread words. This disorder is not a lapse in intelligence; many dyslexic individuals can speak just fine and understand the words and principles. However, they have trouble visually interpreting the writing. Specialized instruction focuses on giving students methods for reading text more carefully to identify what's written.

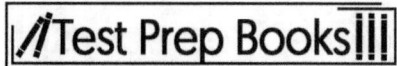

Another type of learning disorder deals with writing difficulties. Students with this type of disorder may read passages without any problems, but when it comes to spelling out words and constructing sentences, there are recurring issues. This difficulty with written expression is called **dysgraphia**, which is characterized by poor handwriting and constant grammatical and spelling errors. While this may seem common in early learners, students with dysgraphia can display these issues at older age ranges. Another core aspect of dysgraphia is that students have difficulties expressing themselves in writing. While they have good ideas, they may have trouble presenting them in a logical sequence. Naturally, the instructor will want to customize the instruction for these students, focusing on writing and composition exercises to address the problem areas and help students regain confidence in their abilities.

It is important to note that disorders cannot be cured the way a doctor might treat an infection. Differentiated instruction can help address some of the core issues of learning disabilities while also boosting student morale. This process will be expedited by keeping students engaged and encouraging them throughout the process; these factors will determine how hard students strive to learn and overcome issues.

Promoting Independent Reading

The following are strategies for promoting purposeful and independent reading of a wide variety of texts:

1. Promote independent reading of narrative, literary, expository, and informational texts.
2. Teach students how to select books that are at appropriate reading levels.
3. Use students' personal interests to help motivate them to read independently.
4. Provide structured reading opportunities in class.
5. Encourage independent reading at home.
6. Monitor students' independent reading.

In addition to teacher read-alouds, students should read independently approximately twenty minutes per day. This time should be structured and occur at predictable times throughout the week. Students should be encouraged to read a variety of texts at this time (narrative, literary, expository, and informational texts).

In order to benefit from independent reading, students must read texts that are appropriate for their assessed reading level. Therefore, students should be aware of their reading levels and be able to select texts that coincide with this level. For students in primary school, the **five-finger test** can be used in the text-selection process. The five-finger test asserts that if a student has trouble with five or more words on a randomly selected page, then the book is above that student's reading level. For older readers, the teacher can group texts into levels and/or categories, from which students can select based on their personal interests.

In order for independent reading time to be effective, students should be accountable for what is read. A great assessment tool is to have each student give an oral report of one book that they have read during the marking period. Students should be given nightly reading homework as well. Teachers may require students to log the number of minutes read each night and have their parents to sign to verify completion.

Students should be given 20 minutes of independent reading time in the classroom each day. Teachers phrase this time as **D.E.A.R.**, or "Drop Everything and Read," time. Students can read a book from home, the library, or one selected from the variety of books found within the classroom.

Teachers are required to have a classroom library. Some schools require a certain number of books or filled bookcases within a classroom. The library center should also contain more than just books. The classroom library should be an inviting environment for students. Small lamps make the area warmer—like home rather than school—and provide extra light for reading. Furniture (such as beanbag chairs, pillows, and small chairs) allows students to get comfortable, rather than reading at their desk. Not only is the environment important, but the classroom library must also be an organized, designated space. If books are disorganized in the classroom library, students may be deterred from using the space appropriately, simply because they cannot find what they are looking for, or out of sheer frustration. Organizing books by theme or genre helps students search for the books they desire. For students in younger grades, books should be grouped in plastic tubs using picture and word category labels like "animals" or "holidays." This organization method is especially helpful for those learning to read.

A listening center is another helpful space in the classroom library. In the listening center, students listen to stories that are played through a sound device (like a CD or MP3 player) and follow along in the text. A teacher can switch the book out weekly to match a theme in the classroom or leave a "free choice bin" for students to choose what they would like to listen to. Again, listening to the story will encourage and emphasize reading strategies, such as voice inflection and pacing.

Having a bookshelf with the teacher's or students' favorite text selections may encourage readers to select a good book quickly. Students like to follow their classmates, so teachers should have a section where students can place books that they can recommend to their friends. Older students can fill out brief recommendation sheets that briefly list a few of a book's main themes so that potential readers can see if they are interested in reading it.

Basic Linguistic Terminology and Concepts Used in Reading Instruction

When teaching reading, there are basic terms and concepts to remember when creating curriculum. Teachers should acknowledge the roles of various language systems and their impact on a child's linguistic development. The earlier children develop strong language skills, the better they will perform throughout their academic years and beyond. As an educator, you can help children develop these skills by working on etymology, vocabulary, grammar knowledge, and sentence structure. Before instructing students, it is crucial that instructors understand the meaning of the following terms.

Phoneme: the individual sound that distinguishes one word from another, e.g., *t*ap, *z*ap, ta*d*.

Morpheme: the meaningful part of a word that cannot be divided into other words; can be standalone words, prefixes, or suffixes, e.g., the morphemes *cat* and *-s* form the word *cats*.

Inflectional suffix: the grammatical ending of a word, e.g., verb present participle ending in *-ing* or a noun plural ending in *-s* or *-es*.

Derivational affix: an affix from which another word is derived; usually combined with a suffix to create a new word, e.g., *delicate* (derivational affix) + *-ly* (suffix) = *delicately*.

Prosody: the pattern of intonation, emphasis, and rhythm when pronouncing syllables.

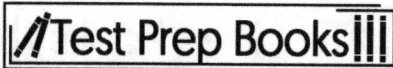

Phonology: the system or organization of sound patterns and their meaning.

Morphology: the formation of words and their relationship to other words.

Syntax: the arrangement and flow of words and phrases to create coherent sentences.

Semantics: the meaning of words, phrases, sentences, and other text.

Discourse: verbal or written exchange of words; means of communication.

Pragmatics: the study of how verbal or written language is communicated within different contexts.

Technology in the Classroom

Technology can be a useful tool in the classroom, but teachers must be careful when integrating it into lessons.

Teach your students how to evaluate material from the internet. Just as teachers need to be aware that some online resources are unreliable, students should learn to recognize high- and low-quality material. Students of all ages can learn age-appropriate lessons about source reliability. For example, you might teach younger students that not every source is reliable by showing them how anyone can edit Wikipedia articles. Evaluating sources is particularly important for older students who are beginning to write research essays. These students can learn the same criteria that teachers use for evaluating research. It may be helpful to go through sources as a class and discuss which ones are reliable.

Be aware that your students will have different degrees of **technological literacy**, which refers to the ability to use electronic devices. For example, a student who knows how to use computers and can easily navigate the internet has high technological literacy; a student who struggles to use electronic devices, on the other hand, has low technological literacy. Children's technological literacy largely depends on their home environment. Some families have computers and allow the students to use them, some students have their own computers, and some lack access altogether. Therefore, you will need to observe each student and offer help to those who are struggling.

Set up parameters to ensure that students' interactions with technology are educational, not distracting. For example, a teacher who is having their students practice writing on a tablet app should ensure that the tablets are locked and will not allow students to exit the app. Otherwise, students will probably waste time playing games instead of practicing their writing.

Foundations of Reading Assessment

Assessments Based on the TEKS for ELAR

In Texas, teachers are required to create curriculum that falls in line with the TEKS for ELAR to prepare students for reading and language arts assessments. These assessments help educators learn the various literacy abilities of their students to inform future instruction. As discussed previously, students' reading skills are directly affected by their environments. Learning the differences in their abilities is key to creating lesson guides.

Teachers should test students at the beginning of the year to determine their initial reading development stages, identify which components of reading they excel in or need help with, and help to determine if a child has special needs.

Because children's reading abilities fluctuate for many reasons, teachers should administer frequent assessments so they can pick up on these changes and adjust their syllabi accordingly. Ongoing assessments help teachers see where their students need improvement. By reviewing test results, an instructor can figure out how to tailor instruction to fit each student's needs.

Obviously, not all testing is standardized. There are regular tests you can give your students to determine their skill levels. Data can and should be collected from these tests to inform curricula. Some of these tests include pop quizzes for vocabulary, free writing, and text recitation. An **Early Diagnostic Reading Assessment (ERDA)** is an informal evaluation that reviews children's knowledge of reading components. You can use ERDA with kindergartners by having them identify and match words and sounds. For children in kindergarten through grade 3, evaluating their ability to recognize letters, syllables, and rhymes is a form of ERDA. Other examples include assessments of recitation and listening comprehension skills.

Regularly testing students' reading and language arts skills has long-term impacts. The earlier their educational needs are realized, the sooner their education can be personalized. Personalized, informed instruction results in higher learning success rates among children.

Types of Assessments

Screening or Entry-Level
Screening assessments are given with the purpose of identifying students who may be at-risk for difficulties in reading. These assessments are typically given at the beginning of the year as students enter into a new grade. They are brief and do not identify lags in specific skills; rather, they simply serve as a way to group students who need intervention to catch them up to grade level.

Formative
Formative assessments are smaller, more informal assessments conducted in the middle of a unit of study. They are meant to determine how students are understanding the material while they are in the process of learning it. Typically, formative assessments should have little to no effect on students' grades. Examples include writing a summary of a text, acting out the plot of a story, drawing a picture that represents the main idea, or completing a "think, pair, share" exercise with a partner. Teachers should use formative assessments to gauge students' understanding and adjust instruction accordingly (e.g., if the majority of the class does not seem to grasp the concept, spend more time on it before moving on).

Summative
Summative assessments should be given at the end of a unit to determine whether students have gained mastery of the content. These assessments often have high point values. Examples include unit tests, midterm or final exams, and large projects.

Diagnostic
Diagnostic assessments are usually given at the beginning of the year, or mid-year when starting a new unit, to determine what students already know about a subject or topic. Teachers can use the results of

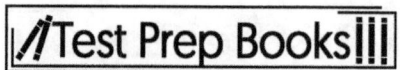

these assessments to inform how they emphasize certain concepts within a unit and to identify any misconceptions students have that need to be addressed. The same assessment can also be given after a particular unit to identify how much progress the students made over the course of instruction; when used this way, it is called a pre- and post- assessment.

Code-Based and Meaning-Based Classroom Reading Assessments

Code-Based Assessments

Letter-Sound Assessments

During phoneme and **letter-sound correspondence assessments**, teachers point to random letters or phonemes. The student is to then say the sound of the letter or phoneme and the teacher records the student's responses. Letter-sound combinations and phonemes with which a student, group, or class needs additional instruction and/or practice can be identified. The teacher can use this information to create lessons that emphasize the identified letter-sound correspondences and/or phonemes.

Phonics Assessments

Examples of ways to test a student's ability to decode words or readily read sight words include Sylvia Green's Informal Word Analysis Inventory, Test of Word Reading Efficacy (TOWRE), and the CORE Phonics Survey. In these types of assessments, students are given a list of words and/or phonics patterns. Initially, high-frequency words that follow predictable phonics patterns are presented. Examples of **predictable phonics patterns** may include blending, word patterns, digraphs, etc. The words presented become more challenging as a student masters less difficult words. For example, a child may be assessed on their ability to decode nonsense words. The nonsense word assessments progress from decoding common sounds to less common sounds. Multisyllabic words within the assessments can reveal how well learners can chunk word parts through syllabication. As with other assessments discussed, the student's responses are recorded on a teacher's record sheet. In this way, the teacher can identify which word analysis principles and sight words a single student, a group of students, or an entire class is having difficulty with. These sight words, word parts, letter combinations, blending patterns, and/or syllabication principles can then be reinforced, retaught, reviewed, and practiced in future lessons. Additionally, the results of the assessment can be used to form instructional groups.

Informal Word Analysis Inventories

These can be used to assess encoding (spelling) of single-syllable words in the traditional manner. Students write the words that are read aloud by their teacher on a sheet of paper. In the early stages of spelling development, students are assessed on lists of words that are common to everyday language, share a word pattern or theme, and/or follow common orthographic patterns. The word lists become more complex as students demonstrate proficiency. The teacher can then plan instruction that targets the letter combinations and patterns with which students are struggling. Such assessments can also be used to form instructional groups of students who share the same approximate developmental stage of spelling to better facilitate differentiated instruction.

As a general rule of thumb, isolated phonics tests should be given every four to six weeks. Spelling assessments can be given weekly or biweekly. Remediation should be implemented when students miss two or more questions on a five-question assessment and three or more questions on a ten-question assessment.

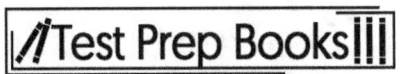

Meaning-Based Assessments

Contextualized Decoding Assessments

Despite the popularity of isolated decoding assessments, decoding should also be assessed in context. The **Word Recognition in Context** subtest of the Phonological Awareness Literacy Screening (PALS) is an example of an assessment that can be used for this purpose. During such assessments, passages that can be read by a student with 90 to 97 percent accuracy at acceptable rates are selected. The student reads these passages aloud to the teacher. By analyzing the student's approach to figuring out unknown words and the student's errors when reading a grade-appropriate passage, teachers are better able to determine which of the following three decoding strategies to emphasize during instruction:

- **Meaning cues** should be emphasized when a student fails to use context, story background, or pictures to assist in the decoding of new words.

- Structural cues are emphasized when a student does not use grammar or syntax to figure out an unknown word.

- Visual cues are emphasized when a student does not use grapheme or phoneme information to decode an unknown word. For example, a student may only read the beginning, middle, or end of words correctly (e.g., read hat as cat). A student may leave off a suffix or use incorrect yet similar letter combinations, indicating that visual cues need to be retaught.

Spelling Assessments

Teachers can assess spelling ability within the context of students' writing samples. This method also enables teachers to detect students' vocabulary, diction, syntax, patterns of misconceptions, and areas that need remediation. Using a rubric can help teachers determine the developmental stage of spelling (pre-phonetic, semiphonetic, phonetic, transitional, or conventional) of each student. Teachers can then create and implement spelling instruction that targets each student's individual strengths, weaknesses, and developmental stage of spelling.

Once a student's areas of need are determined, any of the previously suggested phonics, sight word, or spelling strategies can be used for remediation and re-teaching of the identified skills.

Selecting and Using Diverse Texts

In recent years, there has been a growing emphasis on including diverse texts in the classroom. Diverse texts are books that include characters from minority groups. There are two central reasons for this change. First, students have an easier time relating to characters who share their culture and background; hence, diverse texts help students from minority groups feel included in the classroom and engage with the readings. Diverse texts empower minority students by giving them representation in the classroom, and they also help majority students expand their horizons and develop cultural awareness.

Here are some important criteria to consider when choosing diverse texts for the classroom:

- The book should accurately depict cultural differences. Books that reinforce stereotypes or contain false information will do more harm than good.

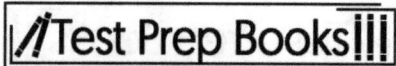

- While the diversity of the students in your classroom can guide your choice of books, it should not limit the scope of literature you choose. Books about any culture in your community, country, or even the world will help students understand and empathize with other people.

- One purpose of diverse literature is to teach children how to correctly interact with people from different cultures. Books should model positive interactions and/or provide meaningful engagement with social issues.

While diverse literature is an essential component of any curriculum, it is best to intersperse these texts with books that feature characters and settings that are familiar to the majority of your students. Since students are most engaged when they can relate to the characters about whom they are reading, not every book needs to be about different cultures.

Teachers should also take their students' interests into account when choosing texts. Consider the surrounding community, as well as any common interests that your students share. Do most of your students live on farms, or are you teaching in an urban community? Are your students always talking about a certain topic or animal? Think about your students' interests, and then choose books that involve those issues.

Characteristics of Standardized Criterion-Referenced and Norm-Referenced Tests

Before you begin administering tests to your students, you should have an understanding of the key assessment concepts and limitations of standardized tests for reading. Assessments should be valid, reliable, and fair.

- **Validity:** The assessment correctly covers the appropriate topic. Only the expected topic is being tested; questions about other subjects are not included.

- **Reliability:** The assessment accurately measures the topic at hand. It consistently analyzes the subject with suitable material and within an adequate time frame.

- **Equity:** The assessment evaluates students' knowledge equivalently. Students are scored on the same scale.

These concepts are often incorporated into two types of standardized tests: criterion-referenced and norm-referenced. Even if all three concepts are taken into account, both types of tests still have limitations when it comes to the detection of reading abilities.

Criterion-referenced tests for reading compare children's reading test scores to proposed standards. This means that the tests are scored based on what students are expected to have learned by certain grade levels. Placement exams are examples of criterion-referenced tests. The results for these tests are usually scored in percentages. These percentages are then categorized into below basic, basic, proficient, and advanced.

Norm-referenced tests contrast children's reading abilities with the expected knowledge of their age group. These tests also rank students' scores in percentiles which are then compared against the expectations for the national, average student. Behavioral screenings and IQ tests are examples of norm-referenced tests.

The intention of these exams is to help teachers determine areas in which students need improvement. However, they can also determine whether or not children can move on to the next grade. Many educators argue that these are not fair assessments; in fact, many teachers and parents have called for an end to standardized testing. Children's cultural, environmental, and socioeconomic status can have a direct effect on their performance, which leaves many at a disadvantage. It is difficult to accurately assess the depth of knowledge in children who may normally require personalized instruction or other assistance with tests.

The ranking methods of these two types of tests could unfairly place students in lower percentiles based on how they performed in one specific area. Remember that no two classrooms are the same—proficient reading levels may differ from one group of similarly aged students to another.

Group and Individual Classroom Reading Assessments

Throughout the school year, reading teachers are responsible for assessing their students' reading abilities. They can do this through individual and group reading assessments.

1. **Individual:** The instructor works with students individually to observe their reading skills.
   Pro: Each student receives special attention; a child with a learning disability may feel at ease when reading alone with the teacher.
   Con: Teachers may not have enough time to spend with each child individually and then teach the entire class.

2. **Group:** The instructor assesses the entire class's reading skills together.
   Pro: Assessing the entire group at once saves the teacher time.
   Con: It is difficult to point out students' individual reading needs.

Formal and Informal Reading Assessments

Overview
Formal assessments, such as selected-response questions, are a useful and quick way to grade students as opposed to free response assessments. However, informal assessments are an even quicker and more frequently used method of assessing students. **Informal assessments** can be conducted after a modeled lesson and before independent practice. The use of individual whiteboards and a few quick selected response questions prepared before the lesson is a quick and helpful tactic for teachers to survey which students grasped the concepts and which students need additional reinforcement. Those who still need to master the skill can then be efficiently identified and grouped together for a small reteach.

Formal Reading Assessments
Standardized reading tests are examples of **formal** assessments that compare and report where students score on a certain scale or in a particular percentile. As mentioned previously, a major drawback to these kinds of tests is that they cannot pick up on students' individual needs; instead, generalizations are made about their reading skills.

Dynamic Indicators of Basic Early Literacy Skills (DIBELS) are another type of formal assessment that measures oral reading fluency. They review children's early reading skills by using methods such as having them read aloud. DIBELS are often used to detect dyslexia and other learning disabilities.

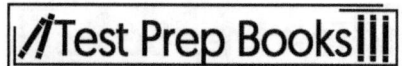

Utilizing the Results of Formal Assessments

When using the results from formal assessments addressing multiple skills, it is important to group students according to ability for the particular skill of interest from the assessment and not just on the overall score. However, the overall score may be beneficial for grouping with regards to pacing and complexity of questions. Lessons and groups should be adjusted to the needs of the students; therefore, student groupings may need to change on a daily or weekly basis. Each student's needs change from concept to concept. Assessments must be ongoing and frequent. Results from these ongoing assessments should be the driving force behind the grouping of students.

Informal Reading Assessments

Informal reading assessments involve direct observation of students' abilities. This can be done via in-class recitations, writing assignments, and special projects. However, it can be difficult for a teacher to accurately determine what learning disabilities their students have via this kind of assessment. Teachers can also be biased toward certain students, which affects how they examine their reading skills.

Instructors can use rubrics to help them analyze children's reading skills by laying out criteria they need to meet at different stages of reading development. Many teachers have created rubrics for reading, writing, and retelling. For example, while having a student retell a story, a teacher can use a rubric to ensure the student is reciting the most important parts of the story.

Core phonics surveys are issued to children in kindergarten through grade 2. **Phonics and spelling surveys** assess students' abilities to recognize the relationship between words and sounds and spell those words accurately as well as determine whether they can define and pronounce certain words. **Reading-error analyses** also test decoding skills; they assess whether students can define unfamiliar terms.

Determining Independent, Instructional, and Frustration Reading Levels

Students should be able to read texts at an independent level with 95% or higher accuracy without assistance. Texts at instructional level should be read with about 90% accuracy; these selections may be difficult for students but nevertheless should be appropriate and discernible with help from the teacher. Finally, students will struggle to read a text at frustration level and will likely experience less than 90% accuracy. Students will find it difficult or impossible to get any meaning out of such texts.

Teachers can determine at which level a student reads a particular text by having the student read aloud a 100-word selection and making note of errors or long hesitations. Subtract the number or errors from the exact number of words in the passage and divide the resulting number by 100 to determine the student's level of fluency. For example, if a student made 10 errors while reading a passage of 100 words, then he or she read 90 words correctly. 90 divided by 100 is equal to .9, or 90%. This would put the text at the instructional level.

Selecting Appropriate Classroom Texts

To find appropriate texts for their classrooms, teachers can consult lists designed to help them choose high-quality materials. Reputable sources of recommendations include reference books, resources provided by your state or school district, and government websites. For example, the Library of Congress offers lists of high-quality books for readers of all ages.

Teachers can also evaluate texts by researching the publisher. Some presses have a record of publishing excellent teaching material; for example, Macmillan/McGraw-Hill and Scholastic both publish high-quality books that are often used in classrooms. Browsing the websites of these and other respected publishers can help you locate good reading material.

Additionally, awards are a useful way of determining whether a book is high quality. For example, the **Newberry Medal** is an annual award that honors the best children's book of the year. The **Horn Book Awards** also judge books for young readers, and they offer awards in categories ranging from picture books to poetry. These are highly competitive awards, so looking at award winners and finalists is a great way to find quality literature. Awards may be particularly useful when vetting books that are only a year or two old, as these texts may not yet appear on reading lists.

Teachers should also choose books that feature age-appropriate topics. Books that include violence or other disturbing content are not good choices for young readers; however, texts that touch on these issues may be useful for older students. For example, a book about the Holocaust would be inappropriate for a first grade classroom, but it could be useful for teaching high school students about history and starting discussions about topics like politics and race.

Illustrations are also an important part of a text, particularly for young readers. The best books have high-quality illustrations that further the meaning of the text instead of detracting from it or confusing readers. Avoid resources with pictures that do not accurately represent the text, as they will mislead students. Drawings that are overly flashy and distracting can also prevent students from focusing on their reading.

Evaluating Text Complexity

Texts should not be too hard or too easy for students. But how can teachers evaluate text complexity to ensure that they are giving their students appropriate materials? There are quantitative and qualitative methods of determining a text's level.

Quantitative measures attempt to objectively calculate the difficulty of a text. The most common quantitative measures are **readability formulas**, or mathematical equations that strive to calculate the difficulty of a text. **Fry's formula** is a common readability formula that requires teachers to count the number of sentences and syllables in three random passages of one hundred words each. They then average each number and chart the two numbers on a Fry graph. The **Fry graph** uses the numbers to produce a suggested grade level for the text. While this method is a useful tool for estimating a text's complexity, teachers should take it with a grain of salt; Fry's formula does not account for variation within grade levels and the text's qualitative factors.

Fry Graph

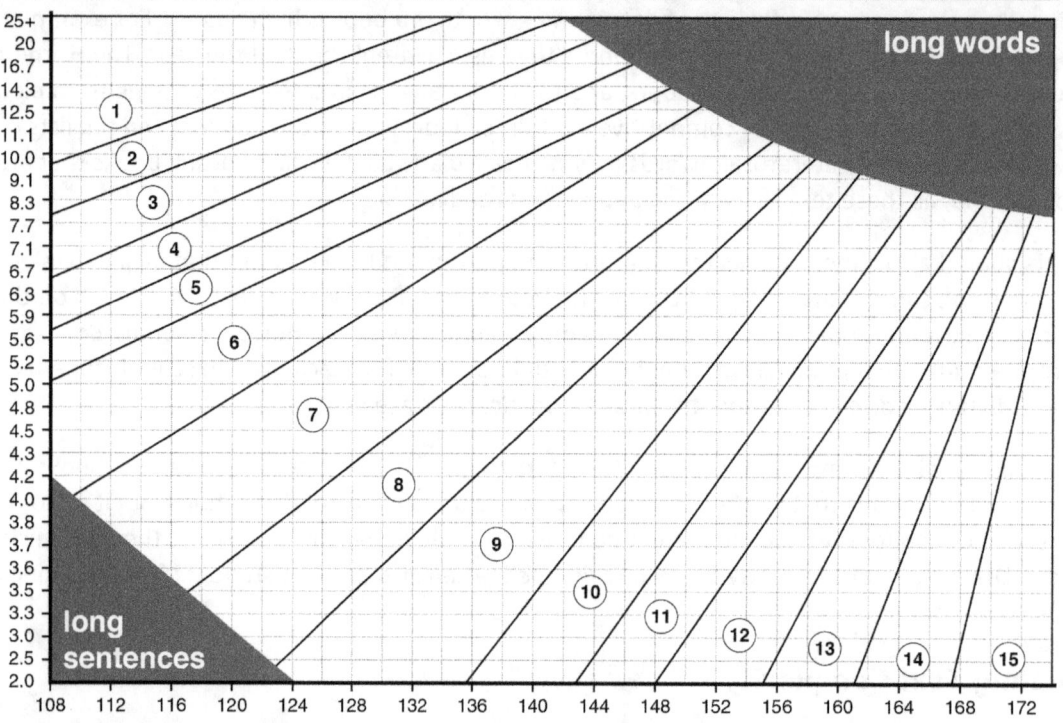

The other common quantitative measures are **Lexile text measures**. Like Fry's formula, these measures rate texts based on sentence length and word complexity. However, the Lexile method uses a database of text rankings instead of having teachers do the math themselves. It also gives texts a numerical rating from 0L to 2000L (L stands for Lexile) instead of a grade level.

Qualitative measures identify subjective elements that affect the text's complexity. Below are some qualitative criteria that teachers can use to determine complexity.

- **Predictable structures** make texts easier to grasp, and they are especially useful in material intended for young children. For example, many fairy tales and children's books repeat questions and phrases. These predictable elements make the text less complicated, as children get into the pattern of the story and do not have to approach each repetition as an entirely new element.

- **Vocabulary** also determines a text's difficulty, and it cannot always be detected by quantitative measures. For example, the word "daft" consists of just one syllable, but it is clearly a more obscure word than "cat." However, Fry's formula would count the two words as the same level. Hence, teachers should skim the material to ensure the vocabulary is at an appropriate level. While texts should include some vocabulary words that will be new to students, an excess of new vocabulary renders reading so frustrating that students are likely to lose interest.

- Teachers should also consider the level of **background knowledge** required to understand a text. If easily learned background information is required (for example, basic historical context), teachers can present it to students before they begin to read a book. But if the background knowledge is complicated or far above the students' grade level, the book is not a good fit.

- Lastly, the **level of meaning** refers to how much abstract thought a text requires. Some texts only require students to understand the literal events of the book. More complex books, however, demand that students use abstract thought to make inferences and evaluate events. High levels of symbolism and abstract thought will be too difficult for younger students, while books that require only literal interpretation will likely seem boring to more mature students.

Engaging Caregivers in Reading Education

Educate caregivers on reading techniques and offer them resources for teaching at home. For example, you could host workshops on teaching phonics so that caregivers know how to help their children sound out words when reading at home. Suggesting supplemental resources for both parents and students is also a great idea. Parents can benefit from recommendations of literacy activities, books to read with their children, or books and websites that teach them how to help their students succeed in reading.

Make opportunities for caregivers to join your classroom. For example, you could have parents come and read aloud to students in class; alternatively, you could invite caregivers who work in fields that relate to your reading to come and answer questions. When parents spend time in the classroom, they gain a better understanding of their child's abilities and needs. Classroom involvement may also inspire caregivers to spend more time working with their children at home.

Communicate regularly with caregivers. Newsletters, parent/teacher meetings, and meetings where the teacher meets with both the parent and the student are all useful. Communication regarding the class's progress and children's individual needs gives caregivers the information they need to help their students succeed. Communication also encourages caregivers to take an active part in their child's education.

Instructional Technologies That Support the Assessment of Reading Development

In an increasingly digitized world, more and more educational resources and supplementary materials can be found online or as easily accessible phone applications. Educators should introduce students to different types of resources and utilize appropriate technology in the classroom to provide students with a variety of ways to further develop their reading skills. However, technological resources do have drawbacks and should be a supplement to, not a replacement of, traditional classroom procedures such as using printed materials and engaging in face-to-face reading instruction.

Hardware that can be utilized for reading development includes laptops/computers, tablets, e-readers, or smartphones. There are many software and application options that are compatible with these devices and can aid in letter recognition, phonics, decoding, and reading fluency, among other things. These resources are constantly being developed and modified, so consider doing regular research into the best and most relevant instructional technologies to incorporate into your classroom.

Benefits to technological instruction and supplementation in the classroom include immediate feedback, individualized practice and differentiation capabilities, aesthetically engaging content, and progress reports that can be reported directly to the teacher.

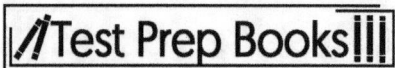

Accommodations in Assessments

Some students may require testing accommodations, which are modifications to the typical testing format. In particular, students with learning disabilities or exceptional challenges may not be able to perform in a way that accurately reflects their understanding of the material due to the conditions under which they are tested. Accommodations are determined by the student's Individualized Education Program (IEP). Examples include extended time, separate setting, administration in multiple/separate sections, and more.

Practice Questions

1. Which of the following is true in Tier 3 interventions?
    a. The entire classroom is assessed using universal screening.
    b. Students who receive Tier 3 support are generally given one-on-one support in addition to classroom teaching.
    c. Progress of Tier 3 instruction is monitored, and many students are able to catch up to grade level effectively.
    d. Many students receive Tier 3 support because their math or reading skills are not quite at grade level.

2. Ability-based differentiation involves which of the following core focus areas?
    a. How students sound out unfamiliar words
    b. How students analyze and use a reading
    c. How students self-select appropriately leveled readings
    d. How students work in peer groups

3. A student takes a standardized formal reading assessment and achieves a score that lands them in the 77th percentile. What does this mean?
    a. The student answered 77 percent of the questions correctly.
    b. The student answered 77 questions correctly.
    c. The student performed better than 77 percent of test takers.
    d. 77 percent of test takers scored higher than the student.

4. If diagnostic assessments indicate students have phonetic problems, which of the following activities would be best for the instructor to introduce?
    a. Activities that analyze the different aspects of words
    b. Activities that help students visualize what they read
    c. Activities that have students paraphrase and summarize texts
    d. Activities that involve using graphic organizers to identify key points and supporting details in texts

5. Which of the following is an example of interest-based differentiation?
    a. Grouping students who are all struggling with comprehending grade-level vocabulary words
    b. Grouping students who are all working on reading fluency
    c. Grouping students who are all working on sounding out unfamiliar words when reading aloud
    d. Grouping students who are all auditory learners

See answers on the next page.

Answer Explanations

1. B: One-on-one support is characteristic of Tier 3 support because this format can provide a more intensive intervention. The rest of the choices more closely describe Tier 1 support.

2. D: Ability-based differentiation addresses three core areas of focus that determine reading proficiency and build reading skills. These include examining students' conceptual understanding of reading, how students analyze and use the reading, and how students evaluate and respond to reading. The other choices describe important skills that students develop, but they are not hallmarks of ability-based differentiation.

3. C: Percentile scores provide a means of score comparison and range from 1 to 99. A student's percentile score indicates the percentage of total test takers that student outperformed. For example, a student who scored in the 77th percentile achieved a score that is higher than 77 percent of the rest of the test cohort. A student's percentile score is different than the percentage of correct responses obtained on the test. A percentile score simply compares one student's score with the scores of all of the other students who took the test.

4. A: When students have phonetic problems, instructors should introduce activities that help the students sound out words and analyze their different aspects to build familiarity with English vocabulary and structure. The other choices would be more appropriate activities to aid reading comprehension.

5. D: Interest-based differentiation is based on the concept that students' performance can be associated with their interest level in the subject or activity. Choices A, B, and C are based on performance or skill level, while Choice D is an example of interest-based differentiation. Instructors can encourage reading growth by allowing students to choose their learning activities. Students more interested in auditory activities may find listening to oral reading exercises more engaging than reading alone in their own head.

Domain II - Reading Development: Foundational Skills

Oral Language Foundations of Reading Development

Oral Language Activities

Oral or spoken language is important when understanding a text. If proficient, a reader's speech will aid their ability to understand and comprehend words, sentences, paragraphs, and a variety of complex texts. Oral language activities, such as purposeful read-alouds, allow students to focus on comprehension skills. Listening skills can promote and serve as a great foundation for comprehension skills. Understanding a text advances students' comprehension skills. When an instructor reads aloud, a student does not need to decode words for fluency. This allows students to listen and focus solely on the text for comprehension. Teacher read-alouds also provide students the opportunity to learn how to emphasize voice and tone while reading.

Developing Communication Skills

Early childhood educators are instrumental in developing effective communication skills in their students. Verbal and nonverbal communication skills are important in setting a positive, educational, supportive environment to optimize learning. They are equally important for students to master for use in their own daily lives. When communicating with others, students should be fully attentive, make eye contact, and use encouraging facial expressions and body language to augment positive verbal feedback. Postures including hands on hips or crossed over the chest may appear standoffish, while smiling and nodding enhance the comfort and satisfaction of the other party. Active listening is the process of trying to understand the underlying meaning in someone else's words, which builds empathy and trust. Asking open-ended questions and repeating or rephrasing in a reflective or clarifying manner is a form of active listening that builds a positive, trusting relationship.

An important skill for children is the ability to communicate effectively with adults; developing this comfort from a young age will be helpful throughout life. Educators can facilitate this through providing experiences where children need to talk to adults in the community. For example, educators may take the class on a field trip to the local community library, where students must ask the librarian for help locating certain health resources. Students might also prepare a health fair and invite parents, community members, and those from senior centers to come learn from posters, demonstrations, and presentations. Children can also work on developing communication skills using an array of technologies such as telephone, written word, email, and face-to-face communication.

Different Learning Styles

In tandem with different communication styles, educators and students alike should be aware of different learning styles. **Auditory learners** learn through hearing, so the educator can use verbal descriptions and instructions. **Visual learners** learn through observation, so the educator can use demonstrations, provide written and pictorial instructional content, and show videos. **Kinesthetic learners** learn through movement, involvement, and experience, so the educator can prepare lessons with hands-on learning, labs, or games with a physical component.

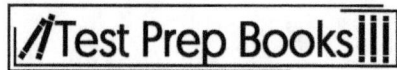

Continuum of Oral Language Development

Before children can speak themselves, they begin the process of oral language development by listening to those around them. When children enter school, they should have an age-appropriate ability to use oral language themselves. As they continue to develop oral language skills, they should first practice listening, then speaking, and finally, conversation. The following guidelines for oral language development are presented in the TEKS for ELAR:

- Students should be able to ask and answer questions based on text or information to which they have listened.
- Students should be able to follow directions that have been given to them orally.
- Students should be able to clearly state their own thoughts verbally.
- Students should be able to engage in casual conversation and discussion with other classmates.

Theories of Language Development

The **Nativist theory of language development** holds that humans learn speech naturally as a result of inborn ability. According to the theory, children naturally have a language acquisition device that enables them to understand and eventually replicate the language. Children are naturally inclined to pick up language. A contrary theory, the **interactionist learning view**, holds that children learn language as a result of their interactions with others. Therefore, the more children are exposed to language, the more they pick up vocabulary and can string together phrases. It is helpful and open-minded to consider that both ideas impact language learning.

Identifying and Supporting Delays in Oral Language Development

An instructor can assess students to see if their issues are based on lack of instruction or erroneous exposure to language, or if a student has a learning disorder that is inhibiting their ability to learn as fluidly as other students. There are several language-related disorders and delays that could make reading difficult for students, so identifying these issues early is key.

Instructors must be patient and engaging as they assess student performance. Hearing how students respond to reading or use spoken language will give indications of what issues are present. For example, students who face difficulties with written English by reversing words or letters or having trouble identifying rhyming words may have common dyslexia. Another common problem is difficulty recognizing letter sounds, which delays students' language progression. All of these issues may occur naturally, interrupting learning ability, but they can be treated through differentiated instruction.

The most effective way to remedy language issues is to identify specific areas of difficulty and provide supplemental instruction. This process is referred to as **articulation therapy**. The first step is isolation, to see if students can make key sounds or help them make the sounds needed for English. Instructors then work to improve the students' understanding of syllables, words, phrases, sentences, reading, and conversation. All of these areas build on each other. Improving English sound production will impact the understanding of syllables and words and therefore pave the way for reading and speaking proficiency.

Important Grammatical Structures Teachers Should Know

Before educators teach reading or writing, they should themselves be masters of the language. They should know the conventions of grammar, punctuation, spelling, and structure of language in order to

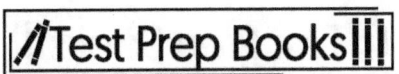

Domain II - Reading Development: Foundational Skills

communicate clearly. They must also be able to interpret what students are saying to either affirm or revise it. Teachers are responsible for differentiating instruction so that students of all levels and aptitudes can succeed with language learning. Teachers need to be able to isolate gaps in skill sets and decide which skills need intervention in the classroom.

Teachers need to have mastery of the conventions of English including:

- Nouns
    - Collective Nouns
    - Compound Subjects
    - Pronouns
    - Subjects, Objects, and Compounds
    - Pronoun/Noun Agreement
    - Indefinite Pronouns
    - Pronoun Reference Problems
    - Noun Plurals
- Adjectives
    - Compound Adjectives
    - Article adjectives
- Verbs
    - Infinitives
    - Verb Tenses
    - Participles
    - Subject/Verb Agreement
    - Active/Passive Voice
- Comparisons
    - Double Comparisons
- Prepositions
    - Prepositional Phrases
- Conjunctions
- Interjections
- Adverbs
- Types of Sentences
- Subjects and Predicates
- Clauses and Phrases
- Misplaced Modifiers
- Dangling Participial Phrases
- Double Negatives
- Capitalization
- Punctuation
    - Periods
    - Commas
    - Semicolons and Colons
    - Parentheses and Dashes
    - Quotation Marks
    - Apostrophes
    - Hyphens

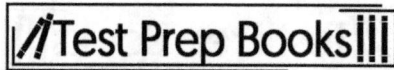

Domain II - Reading Development: Foundational Skills

- o Question Marks
- o Exclamation Points
- Spelling
  - o Spelling Hurdles
  - o Homonyms and other easy mix-ups
- Prefixes and Suffixes
- Abbreviations
- Pronunciation

Teaching Grade-Level Language to Label and Describe

Teaching children how to label people, places, objects, and other categories does not have to be hard. When children learn words, they are often taught to associate those words with particular objects. Using grade-level instructional language to increase students' labeling skills is integral.

Start with simple, everyday items that students already encounter. Point to the items, say what they are, and ask the class to repeat. Then practice pointing at the items and asking students to say what they are. You can also do the reverse, by naming the items and asking the students to point them out. Play a game like I Spy by saying, "I spy something blue," and see what children notice around the classroom.

Hang up a picture of something they encounter often, like a school bus. Label the bus with its name, and then ask students to describe it, putting those descriptive labels around it (such as "big," "yellow," and "loud"). Incorporate other places and actions into this exercise by asking the class where the bus goes, who rides it, and what the bus driver does. Repeat this process with other objects, like blankets, fruit, books, or toys in the classroom. Pass around the toys and ask the students what they feel like, so they can learn to describe textures.

Once the students have participated in labeling the objects, teach them to form full sentences describing these or other items. Perhaps they can even write out short stories accompanied by drawings. Ask them to describe their outfits, the instructor's appearance, and their pets, to name a few things. Reinforce children's knowledge of actions by having them perform some in class. Simon Says is a good game to use when teaching students to label actions and parts of the body.

Once students can label objects they're familiar with, introduce them to new things. This can be done by showing them an educational program like Sesame Street. Pause the video to quiz the children about what they have just seen. Call on them individually and tell them to describe what they saw in complete sentences like, "Oscar the Grouch is green. He lives in a trash can."

Labeling people, objects, and actions takes practice. With the right activities, children will learn to do it successfully.

Oral Language and Reading Comprehension Development

Oral language is also important when learning reading comprehension. Reviewing and identifying new and key vocabulary prior to reading the text help students understand the text more efficiently. Once students are familiar with new vocabulary words, they should be able to interpret the word in context of the reading, rather than reaching the word and skipping over the sentence or needing to stop and look up the word before continuing to read. Previewing text and skimming pictures for younger students, or reviewing bold subtitles for older students, can benefit students' comprehension by helping to gain an idea of what the text may be about before reading. There are different ways to find a text's purpose using auditory and speech skills, some of which include summarizing with a peer or paraphrasing the text.

When students are paired together or placed in small groups, they can share and discuss elements of texts. Literature circles are like book clubs. These circles allow students to speak freely, create their own discussions, and form questions about the text. Teachers can provide literature circle booklets, which may contain response or discussion questions to enhance conversation within the group.

Standard American English and Its Deviations

Inevitably, all languages deviate from their standard format. In America, Standard American English has evolved into different forms (**dialects**) that are spoken across the country based on cultural influences and location. These dialects, while still considered English, are not Standard English. This is because some of the grammar, pronunciations, or general phonetics are inconsistent with the designated standard. Whether students are native English speakers or learning English as a second language, learning Standard English will give them a holistic understanding of American language conventions.

Students have likely encountered examples of American English deviation before, so the risk here is that they think slang or idiomatic choices reflect correct English usage. It is important to review English language structure frequently to ensure students know the proper pronunciations of words and how sentences fit together. However, this still does not eliminate confusion with hearing other English dialects; after all, these dialects are still English. One way to teach students Standard American English is to illustrate the difference between the standard form and other dialects.

Citing specific examples of dialectic English that deviate from the standard is key. For example, Americans living in the South tend to use the word *y'all* to summarize the phrase *you all*. *Y'all* isn't recognized as part of Standard American English, so the correct version is *you all*. Distinctions such as this will help students visualize and hear proper English in use, which will help them recognize and use Standard English when reading and speaking.

In addition to reviewing proper word use and phonetics, training should also incorporate pronunciation. Writing and reading Standard English is very important, but students should also know the correct way to say the words they're reading. In addition to explaining pronunciation rules, instructors can periodically ask students to say and pronounce random words in a reading passage to test their skills. Visualization activities and tools will also help. Flash cards with pronunciation guides for keywords are just one way to help students pronounce difficult vocabulary words.

Making Cross-Language Connections

Students may come from non-English speaking homes or backgrounds. Though they may not be native English speakers, certain vocabulary words or grammatical concepts may be similar to their language of origin. Teachers should creatively engage such students by making English seem relevant to them; this can be done by making connections to root words/derivatives, utilizing diverse illustrations, or allowing the student(s) to share words or phrases from their native language with the class and comparing them to the English equivalents.

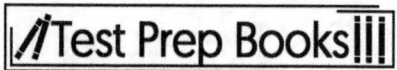

Basic Concepts Related to Second-Language Acquisition

There are many factors that influence a child's language acquisition. A child's physical age, level of maturity, home and school experiences, general attitudes toward learning, and home languages are just some of the many influences on a child's literacy development. However, a child's **language acquisition** progresses through the following generalized stages.

Stage	Examples	Typical Age
Preproduction	Does not verbalize/nods yes and no	Zero to six months
Early production	One-to-two-word responses	Six to twelve months
Speech emergence	Produces simple sentences	One to three years
Intermediate fluency	Simple to more complex sentences	Three to five years
Advanced fluency	Near-native level of speech	Five to seven years

While this applies to language acquisition in one's home language, the same stages apply to English learners (ELs). Since effective communication in any given language requires much more than a mere collection of vocabulary words that one can accurately translate, it is imperative to pay particular attention to each stage in language acquisition. In addition to vocabulary knowledge, language acquisition involves the study and gradual mastery of intonation, a language's dialects, and the various nuances in a language regarding word use, expression, and cultural contexts. With time, effort, patience, and effective instructional approaches, both students and educators will begin to see progress in language acquisition.

Second language acquisition does not happen overnight. When educators take the time to study each stage and implement a variety of effective instructional approaches, progress and transition from one stage to the next will be less cumbersome and more consistent. In the early stages of language acquisition, children are often silently observing their new language environment. At these early stages, listening comprehension should be emphasized with the use of read alouds, music, and visual aids. Educators should be mindful of their vocabulary usage by consciously choosing to speak slowly and to use shorter, less complex vocabulary. Modeling during these beginning stages is also very effective. If the educator has instructed the class to open a book, the educator can open a book as a visual guide. If it is time to line up, the educator can verbally state the instruction and then walk to the door to begin the line.

During the **pre-production stage**, educators and classmates may assist ELs by restating words or sentences that were uttered incorrectly, instead of pointing out errors. When modeling the correct language usage instead of pointing out errors, learners may be less intimidated to practice their new language.

As students progress into the **early production stage**, they will benefit from exercises that challenge them to produce simple words and sentences with the assistance of visual cues. The educator should ask students to point to various pictures or symbols and produce words or sentences to describe the images they see. At the early production and **speech emergent stages**, EL students are now ready to answer more diverse questions as they begin to develop a more complex vocabulary. Working in pairs or small groups with native speakers will help ELL students develop a more advanced vocabulary.

At the beginning and **intermediate fluency stages**, ELs may be asked questions that require more advanced cognitive skills. Asking for opinions on a certain subject or requiring students to brainstorm and find ways to explain a given phenomenon are other ways to strengthen language proficiency and increase vocabulary.

When a child reaches the **advanced fluency stage**, they will be confident in social and academic language environments. This is an opportune time to introduce and/or increase their awareness of idiomatic expressions and language nuances.

World-Class Instructional Design and Assessment (WIDA) is a consortium of various departments of education throughout the United States that design and implement proficiency standards and assessments for English and Spanish language learners. Primarily focusing on listening, speaking, reading, and writing, WIDA has designed and implemented English language development standards and offers professional development for educators, as well as educational research on instructional best practices. The five English language proficiency standards according to WIDA are as follows:

- Within a school environment, ELL students require communication skills for both social and instructional purposes.

- Effective communication involving information, ideas, and concepts is necessary for ELL students to be academically successful in the area of Language Arts.

- Effective communication involving information, ideas, and concepts is necessary for ELL students to be academically successful in the area of Mathematics.

- Effective communication involving information, ideas, and concepts is necessary for ELL students to be academically successful in the area of Science.

- Effective communication involving information, ideas, and concepts is necessary for ELL students to be academically successful in the area of Social Studies.

According to WIDA, mastering the understanding, interpretation, and application of the four **language domains**—listening, speaking, reading, and writing—is essential for language proficiency. Listening requires ELL students to be able to process, understand, interpret, and evaluate spoken language. Speaking proficiently allows ELL students to communicate their thoughts, opinions, and desires orally in a variety of situations and for a variety of audiences. The ability to read fluently involves the processing, understanding, interpreting, and evaluating of written language with a high level of accuracy, and writing proficiency allows ELL students to engage actively in written communication across a multitude of disciplines and for a variety of purposes.

Since language acquisition involves the ELL students, their families, their classmates, educators, principals and administrators, as well as test and curriculum developers, WIDA strives to ensure that the English Language Proficiency Standards reflect both the social and academic areas of language development.

The Four English Language Proficiency Levels

Children who are learning English or speak it as a second language should be given tailored instruction. According to the Texas English Language Proficiency Standards (ELPS), there are four language proficiency levels:

- Beginner: Learners who do not recognize most spoken English

- Intermediate: Learners who are familiar with some frequently spoken English

- Advanced: Learners who have a good grasp of English and are able to understand it in classroom instruction with some assistance

- High advanced: Learners who can understand English in and out of the classroom with minimal support and are mostly fluent

Remember that each grade level in elementary school usually has a list of sight words that students should know. Beginners will likely need help recognizing the first level of these words. Understand that these students will most likely be silent in class. To instruct them, associate sight words and other frequently used vocabulary with visuals.

Visuals also help intermediate English learners. These students will be more familiar with common English words, but you can still help them advance by giving instructions slowly and using verbal cues. Breaking the classroom into smaller groups when doing reading activities can also be helpful, as English learners are more likely to ask questions when they are not being pressured to speak in front of the entire class.

Advanced and high advanced students can be taught with similar techniques. Since these students are nearly fluent, they most likely will not need sight word exercises. They can be put into groups with children who are at an equal or higher level of English-speaking and reading, which fosters peer support. These students should be issued regular assessments, like vocabulary tests and writing assignments, to give teachers an idea where they need further improvement. Recitation exercises are also useful for hearing whether they are pronouncing words correctly.

Culturally Responsive Instruction

The classroom must be a place that emphasizes respect for all individuals as well as collaboration to achieve a successful learning environment. In addition to teaching reading skills, the instructor is expected to be a model of tolerance and inclusiveness for all students, thus encouraging them to be open-minded toward others. In the United States, it is likely that instructors will have students from a broad range of cultural and linguistic backgrounds. Obviously, these students must be made to feel welcome, and any linguistic difficulties they have should be treated as simply another step in the learning process, not as a result of their background. Any difficulty is an opportunity for the whole class to learn and grow.

Encouraging polite and respectful behavior is key. An instructor does not necessarily need to explain polite behavior, but rather should serve as a role model for the class. When addressing students' issues, the teacher should be sensitive to how they feel and be encouraging no matter their religious or ethnic background. It is also important to monitor how students act and respond to one another. Proper language and behavior should be enforced when necessary, and rude, insensitive language or behavior must be addressed and corrected. Teachers should simultaneously emphasize diversity, equality, and respect for all. When disrespect occurs, steps should be taken to ensure that it is not repeated. It is important to remember that behaviors and lessons in early learners will inform how children grow and mature.

Reading and writing activities can also provide lessons in respect and collaboration. For instance, students can do group work on a text that discusses respectful behavior. Other lessons can look at readings from different cultures to expand the students' appreciation and interest in diversity.

Differentiating Instruction in Oral Language Development

Oral language skills are important for students to have in order to thrive in an English-speaking environment. Beyond comprehending spoken English, understanding oral language structure helps students comprehend the context of what they are reading and how to respond appropriately. All languages utilize grammar, vocabulary, phonology, morphology, discourse, and pragmatics; these concepts combine to form effective communication.

As an instructor, it is important to be mindful of how comfortable the class is with oral language. Native English speakers may be more proficient than those who are learning English as a second language; the latter may need more differentiated instruction to build their conceptual knowledge. No matter the range of student experiences, reading instructors should incorporate drills and lessons that frequently review oral language components throughout the course, which will ensure that core skills such as grammar and word formation remain fresh in students' minds as they continue to progress in reading proficiency. This can be done in a variety of ways using both teacher-based and student-based grouping instruction.

Strategically, it is best to promote oral language by having students isolate and identify different aspects of sentences such as grammar and even vocabulary terms. Reviewing **phonology**, the sounds of English, and **morphology**, how words are formed, is also important. One way to review these aspects would be to present a sample of text and then have students deconstruct the sentences to identify these structures.

Discourse, which studies how language is used in communication, and **pragmatics**, which reflects the correct use of the language, can be reviewed through text examination and interactive activities. It is important to alter and differentiate instruction to review reading principles in different ways and expand critical-thinking skills. One method for reviewing discourse and pragmatics would be for the instructor to write or speak a sentence and then have the class discuss the discourse and pragmatics together. Students can also create the sentences themselves, demonstrating their ability to replicate correct language structure and recognize incorrect sentence components. When reviewing language structure, instructors should continue to assess how students are grasping the material and monitor progress. It is important to remember that reading improvements begin with a strong understanding of language fundamentals.

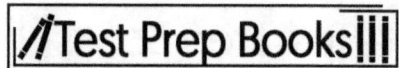

Domain II - Reading Development: Foundational Skills

Phonological and Phonemic Awareness

Phonological and Phonemic Awareness

Phonological awareness is the recognition that oral language is made of smaller units, such as syllables and words. Phonemic awareness is a type of phonological awareness. Phonemic-aware students recognize specific units of spoken language called phonemes. **Phonemes** are unique and easily identifiable units of sound. Examples include /t/, /b/, /c/, etc. It is through phonemes that words are distinguished from one another.

Phonemic Awareness in Reading Development

Phonological and phonemic awareness do not require written language because phonemic awareness is based entirely upon speech. However, phonological and phonemic awareness are the prerequisites for literacy. Thus, experts recommend that all kindergarten students develop phonemic awareness as part of their reading preparation.

Once students are able to recognize phonemes of spoken language, phonics can be implemented in grades K–2. Phonics is the direct correspondence between and blending of letters and sounds. Unlike phonemic awareness, **phonics** requires the presence of print. Phonics often begins with the alphabetic principle, which teaches that letters or other characters represent sounds. Students must be able to identify letters, symbols, and individual sounds before they can blend multiple sounds into word parts and whole words. Thus, phoneme awareness and phonics predict outcomes in word consciousness, vocabulary, reading, and spelling development.

Relevant Vocabulary

- **Word boundaries:** Students must be able to identify how many letters are in a word and that spaces separate words.

- **Onset:** An onset is the beginning sound of any word. For example, /c/ is the onset in the word *cat*.

- **Rime:** The rime of a word is the sound that follows its onset. The /at/ is the rime in *cat*.

- **Syllables:** A syllable is a unit of speech that contains a vowel sound. A syllable does not necessarily have to be surrounded by consonants. Therefore, every syllable has a rime. However, not every syllable has an onset.

- **Syllabification:** Syllabification is the dividing of words into their component syllables.

- **Rhyming words:** Rhyming words are often almost identical except for their beginning letter(s). Therefore, rhyming is an effective strategy to implement during the analytic phase of phonics development.

Phonemic Awareness Skills
Phoneme Recognition

Phoneme recognition occurs when students recognize that words are made of separate sounds and they are able to distinguish the initial, middle, and final phonemes within words. Initial awareness of phonemes should be done in isolation and not within words. Then, phoneme awareness can be

Domain II - Reading Development: Foundational Skills

achieved through shared readings that are supplemented with identification activities, such as the identification of rhyming words.

Blending

Sound blending is the ability to mix together two or more sounds or phonemes. For example, a **consonant blend** is a combination of two or more consonants into a single sound such as /ch/ or /sh/. Blending often begins when the teacher models the slow pronunciation of sound parts within a word. Students are to do likewise, with scaffolding provided by the teacher. Eventually, the pronunciation rate is increased, so that the full word is spoken as it would be in normal conversation.

Segmenting

Sound segmentation is the ability to identify the component phonemes in a word. Segmentation begins with simple, single-syllable words. For instance, a teacher might pronounce the word tub and see if students can identify the /t/, /u/, and /b/ sounds. The student must identify all three sounds in order for sound segmentation to be complete.

Deleting

Sound deletion is an oral activity in which one of the phonemes of a spoken word is removed. For example, a teacher may say a word aloud and then ask students to say the word without a specific sound (e.g., "What word would be formed if cat is said without the /c/ sound?"). With repetition, deletion activities can improve phoneme recognition.

Substituting

Like deletion, **substitution** takes place orally and is initiated through modeling. However, instead of deleting a phoneme or syllable, spoken words are manipulated via the substitution of one phoneme for another (e.g., "What word would be formed if we change the /b/ in bun to /r/?").

Strategies for Developing Phonemic Awareness

A child demonstrates phonemic awareness when identifying rhymes, recognizing alliterations, and isolating specific sounds inside a word or a set of words. Students who demonstrate basic phonemic awareness will eventually also be able to blend together a variety of phonemes independently and appropriately.

Some classroom strategies to strengthen phonemic awareness may include:

- Introduction to nursery rhymes and word play
- Introduces speech discrimination techniques to train the ear to hear more accurately
- Repeated instruction connecting sounds to letters and blending sounds
- Use of visual images coupled with corresponding sounds and words
- Teaching speech sounds through direct instruction
- Comparing known and unfamiliar words
- Practicing pronunciation of newly introduced letters, letter combinations, and words
- Practicing word decoding
- Differentiating similar sounding words

Age-appropriate and developmentally appropriate instruction for phonological and phonemic awareness is key to helping children strengthen their reading and writing skills. Phonological and

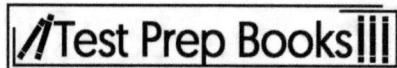

Domain II - Reading Development: Foundational Skills

phonemic awareness, or PPA, instruction works to enhance correct speech, improve understanding and application of accurate letter-to-sound correspondence, and strengthen spelling skills. Since skill-building involving phonemes is not a natural process, PPA instruction is especially important for children who have limited access and exposure to reading materials and who lack familial encouragement to read. Strategies that educators can implement include leading word and sound games, focusing on phoneme skill-building activities, and ensuring all activities focus on the fun, playful nature of words and sounds instead of rote memorization and drilling techniques.

Impact of Phonological and Phonemic Awareness in Literacy Development

Because English is an alphabetic language, phonological and phonemic awareness are foundational skills for any aspect of English language development. Students learning to read need to have an understanding that each letter represents a sound and that those letters and sounds come together to form words that have meaning.

Many studies have shown that children who struggle with phonological or phonemic awareness early on will later struggle with reading and spelling. Therefore, it is of utmost importance to emphasize these skills and target students who need additional assistance.

Letter-Sound Correspondences

When children begin to learn the various letter-sound correspondences, their phonemic awareness begins to overlap with their awareness of orthography and reading. One of the widely accepted strategies to employ when introducing children to letter-sound correspondences is to begin with those correspondences that occur the most frequently in simple English words. In an effort to help build confidence in young learners, educators are encouraged to introduce only a few letter-sound combinations at a time and provide ample opportunities for practice and review before introducing new combinations. Although there is no formally established order for the introduction of letter-sound correspondences, educators are encouraged to consider the following general guidelines. However, they should also keep in mind the needs, experiences, and current literacy levels of the students. The following is intended as a general guide only:

1. a	6. n	11. g	16. l	21. x
2. m	7. c	12. h	17. e	22. v
3. t	8. d	13. i	18. r	23. y
4. p	9. u	14. f	19. w	24. z
5. o	10. s	15. b	20. k	25. j
				26. q

As a generally accepted rule, short vowels should be introduced ahead of long vowels, and uppercase letters should be mastered before the introduction of their lowercase counterparts.

Interactive Activities to Teach Phonemic Awareness

There are approximately forty-four phonemes in the English language. Children begin learning phonemic awareness before they enter grade school. Children who struggle with phonemic awareness skills tend to have a hard time learning to read and may even have reading disabilities.

The following are interactive teaching strategies you can use to further develop the students' skills in phonemic awareness:

- Recognizing and sounding out syllables is one way to teach phonemes to small children. Do this by dividing up a common word like "begin." Sound the word out and ask students to repeat it slowly.

- Using visuals is a very popular technique used by many teachers. Assign images to phonemes, and then combine them to create words. See if the students can guess which words are being created.

- You can ask children to count the words in a sentence. Write out a sentence on the board, and then ask students to repeat it. After they've done this, ask them how many words are in that sentence. Repeat with a new phrase.

- Matching words that rhyme is another great tactic. This can also be done with images or alphabet blocks. For example, children can be asked to spell out words that end in "-un." See if they can come up with matching terms like "fun," "run," "bun," and so forth. Try this with other common endings.

- Something as basic as sounding out individual phonemes is important. You can select from the entire list of phonemes (or go over a few each day) and ask children to repeat them multiple times. Observe how they are pronouncing them. When it appears that they've mastered one phoneme, move on to the next.

Supporting English Learners and Speakers of Various Dialects or Regional Styles

Teachers should keep in mind that the standard English instruction students receive at school may not be reinforced outside of the classroom. For example, there are students who speak English as a second language or simply do not speak English at home. In addition, some native English speakers converse in a variety of dialects and regional styles. Taking this into account, there are ways to support and cater to children that fall into these categories when teaching English phonemes.

There are some sounds in the English language that are not present in other languages. To demonstrate connections between languages, teachers can cover cognates, which are words that are similarly spelled, defined, and pronounced in different languages. To reinforce the English alphabet, spend extra time on alphabet pronunciation. See which letters students are able to recognize already and note which ones they show unfamiliarity with. Associating these unfamiliar letters with pictures is extremely helpful.

Similar strategies are also helpful for English speakers who use various dialects. Some regional dialects drop certain letters from words or utilize alternative pronunciations. Make lists of words your particular group of students may have difficulty pronouncing and have the students practice writing and reciting each term. Focus on vowel sounds in these words, having students repeat them accordingly.

Rigorous study of phonemes should be implemented with both students of varying dialects and non-native English speakers. Beginning in first grade, frequent practice with sentence structure, vocabulary, and recitation should take place.

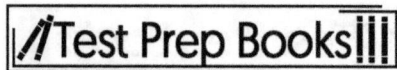

Children that already know how to read in their native languages may be easier to instruct than those who do not. This is because these children have learned how to recognize specific phonemes in their languages in order to read effectively. If they are still struggling, draw specific terms from the texts you are reading in class and spend a significant amount of time on those terms to help students decode.

Differentiating Instruction in Phonological and Phonemic Awareness Skills

When delving into phonological and phonemic awareness, teachers need to consider the varying needs of their students. Some children will have higher literacy skills while others will still be struggling with basic phonemes. The instructor should have observed these variances through regular assessments. Below are some best practices for differentiating instruction to address all students' needs.

Break Students into Small Groups
Some students love speaking up in front of the entire class, while others are more reluctant. The latter may feel more comfortable working in pairs of two or in small groups of three to four students.

How students are paired can vary. Students can be grouped with others who share the same phonemic awareness levels, or they can be mixed. Sometimes pairing a student who is struggling with phonemic awareness with one who is more knowledgeable can improve their overall performance.

Decode a Variety of Words
Remember that some students will be able to decode better than others. However, to cover the bases with all students, start with simple terms and gradually include more difficult ones. Whether you start by teaching a book from a lower grade or going back to basics like sight word flashcards, present students with different words and provide assignments to help them grasp those terms. Spelling and vocabulary tests are especially useful for these tasks.

Use Segmentation
Segmenting words and phrases helps children at all levels work on their pronunciation and their knowledge of sentence structure. For example, teachers can start with simple words that most children should know by that particular grade. Say the word very slowly and ask the children to spell it. Have them identify each of the word's distinct sounds. Move on to more advanced words. After this, move on to sentences. Associate each word in a sentence with a beat, like a tap on the table. With each word, have the children tap when they recite them. Then ask them how many words were in that sentence. If they are already reading, ask them to identify the sentence structure (noun, adjective, verb, etc.).

It is impossible to suit every child's needs perfectly. The more student needs are monitored, the more teachers can create lessons that cater to them.

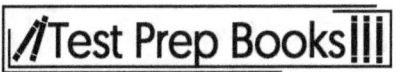

Print Concepts and Alphabet Knowledge

Print Awareness

Print awareness, the understanding that printed words carry meaning, aids reading development. Print awareness includes the understanding that:

1. Words are made of letters, spaces appear between words, and words make sentences.

2. Print is organized in a particular way (e.g., read from left to right and top to bottom, read from front to back, etc.).

3. Different types of print serve specific purposes (magazines, billboards, essays, fiction, etc.).

Print awareness provides the foundation on which all other literacy skills are built. It is often the first stage of reading development. Print awareness helps students develop skills such as word reading, reading comprehension, and letter-sound correspondence. For this reason, a child's performance on tasks relevant to their print awareness is indicative of the child's future reading achievement.

The following strategies can be used to increase print awareness in students:

1. *An adult reads aloud to students or conducts shared reading experiences.* In order to maximize print awareness within the student, the reader should point out the form, function, orientation, and sounds of letters and words.

2. *Utilize shared reading experiences as a tool for building one-to-one correspondence.* **One-to-one correspondence** is the ability to match written letters or words to a spoken word when reading. This can be accomplished by pointing to words as they are read. This helps students make text-to-word connections. Pointing also aids **directionality**, or the ability to track the words that are being read.

3. *Use the child's environment.* To reinforce print awareness, teachers can make a child aware of print in their environment, such as words on traffic signs. Teachers can reinforce this by labeling objects in the classroom.

4. *Instruct students about book organization during read-alouds.* Students should be taught the proper orientation, tracking, and numbering conventions of books. For example, teachers can differentiate the title from the author's name on the front cover of a book.

5. *Let students practice.* Allowing students to practice book-handling skills with wordless books, predictable text, or patterned text will help to instill print awareness.

Print Concepts

By kindergarten, most students will have been exposed to print in the form of books, magazines, and other mediums. Assessment of print concepts will determine whether or not students understand that the print sources they have been exposed to contain meaning. To do this, the teacher can ask students to identify book titles, individual words, and sentences. They should also make note of whether the students associate the words being read with speech.

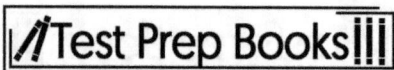

Print concepts involve recognition of the stories being told, punctuation used, and basic things like the parts of a book. For students with cultural barriers, learning the direction in which the text should be read is also a print concept.

Alphabet Knowledge

School-aged children should be familiar with the recitation of the alphabet. This common group activity is not great at determining how many letters individual students know, however. Conduct follow-up assignments to track individual students' progress. One way to do this is by focusing on a group of letters each day and reviewing the sounds of those letters. After having the students associate the letters and sounds, give them writing or spelling assignments to enforce the concept. Have them practice writing the letters in uppercase and lowercase and ask them to spell out the sounds they've heard.

Alphabet puzzles and blocks are inexpensive and available in many stores; give these to students to put together to further familiarize them with letters. Spell simple words with them like "bat," sounding out each letter of the word, and then ask the children to re-create them with their blocks.

Alphabetic Principle

The **alphabetic principle** is the understanding of the names and sounds produced by letters, letter patterns, and symbols printed on a page. Through the alphabetic principle, students learn letter-sound correspondence, phonemic awareness, and the application of simple decoding skills such as the sounding out and blending of letter sounds. Since reading is essentially the blending together of multiple letter sounds, the alphabetic principle is crucial in reading development.

The first part of the alphabetic principle is realizing that words are made up of letters that represent sounds. Careful instruction is needed here. Break down the letters and sounds into groups of consonants and vowels. Make a plan for how many you want to go over each week. Eventually, combine the sounds into commonly used words.

Recoding is the second part of the alphabetic principle; this is when the letters in printed words are interpreted into sounds. Teachers usually start teaching spelling once their students understand the process of recoding. Spelling is as important to the alphabetic principle as it is to reading. Prepare spelling activities, such as word games, where the students have to recreate the new words that they have learned.

Research has revealed the following sequence to be effective when teaching the alphabetic principle:

1. Letter-sound relationships need to be taught explicitly and in isolation. The rate at which new letter-sound correspondences can be presented will be unique to the student group. Letter-sound pairs that are used frequently should be presented before letter-sound pairs with lower utility. Similarly, letter-sound pairs that can be pronounced in isolation without distortion (*f, m, s, r*) should be presented first. Instruction of letters that sound similar should not be presented in proximity.

2. Once single-letter and sound combinations are mastered, consonant blends and clusters (*br, ch, gr*) can be presented.

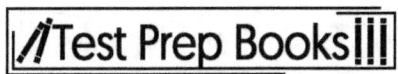

Promoting Children's Development of the Alphabetic Principle

When teaching the concepts of the alphabetic principle, start with the letters themselves. Many students will be familiar with the alphabet through the ABCs song. Then practice the sounds of each letter, ensuring that the students make proper associations between the letter and its sound(s). Consider going in alphabetical order, sounding out a few letters a day. A chart can be displayed with each letter's respective sounds written out.

Combine the letters with common phonemes to make different words. Play a matching game. Have a group of single letters on one side and phonemes on the other. See how many words students can come up with on their own.

Because students learn at different levels, use differentiation and intervention strategies when teaching these concepts. You want to encourage students to learn at their own pace. Teaching guided reading in small teams and or individually is a helpful strategy. Setting individual goals for how much each student should learn each week is another. Intervention usually applies to students that need a little extra help. They may be placed in special education programs to help them learn further.

Teachers should have patience with students as they develop their knowledge of the alphabet and the alphabetic principle. To help students master the alphabetic principle, instructors should spend a great deal of time teaching the relationships between letters and sounds.

Taking the time to reinforce instruction should be part of every lesson plan. To reinforce knowledge of the alphabetic principle, teachers can use articulatory feedback and writing exercises using phonetic spelling.

Articulatory, or auditory, feedback occurs when a person speaks into a device that records and plays back what they said to ensure they are saying it correctly. With the alphabetic principle, teachers can have students participate in articulatory feedback to make sure they are pronouncing letters correctly. By teaching them to pronounce correctly, this process actually helps children speak fluently, with the appropriate tone and pitch. Auditory feedback devices are commonly used to help those who stutter.

Recite different combinations of letters and vowels out loud. Read a list of phonemes and ask students to write how they think they are spelled. Start to blend different sounds together and see if students can identify them all. This exercise is not about spelling, but it will be interesting for the teacher to see how creative students are when they visualize sounds.

After conducting these exercises, have students perform a short writing exercise. See how learning to pronounce words correctly and working on phonetic spelling affects their overall writing skills.

Print Concepts, Alphabet Knowledge, and the Alphabetic Principle

Children's alphabet knowledge will increase right along with their awareness of print concepts and the alphabetic principle. The TEKS for ELAR specify the skills students should continue developing between kindergarten and third grade.

Between kindergarten and third grade, students should progress through the following print concepts:

1. Identify the physical components of books
2. Hold printed material in the correct position

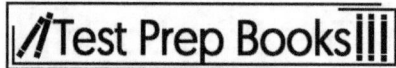

3. Recognize word spacing and boundaries
4. Know the difference between upper and lowercase letters
5. Learn to use dictionaries, thesauruses, and other print or digital mediums to define words

Students' alphabet knowledge should develop as follows:

1. Arrange words in alphabetical order
2. Find words in the correct part of the dictionary or glossary
3. Spell increasingly complex words
4. Decode words with unusual vowel sounds
5. Write letters in both print and cursive

To demonstrate the continuum of development of the alphabetic principle, children in grades K-3 should be able to:

- Create words from letters and phonemes
- Segment words into phonemes
- Recognize syllables
- Match letters with sounds
- Recognize prefixes and suffixes

These are just a few of the skills that should be continually developed as children progress through third grade. The purpose of these guidelines is to help teachers make appropriate lesson plans. As always, keep in mind that not all students will develop these skills at the same pace, so you will need to adjust your plans accordingly.

Assessing Print Awareness and Alphabet Knowledge

Entry-level assessments, progress monitoring, and summative assessments need to be administered in order to determine students' print awareness, letter recognition, and alphabetic principle knowledge to identify misconceptions that can be remediated in future lessons. Formal and informal assessment methods are as follows:

- **Print awareness** is easily assessed through observation. Teachers can give students a book and ask them to demonstrate their tracking and orientation knowledge. Similarly, teachers can ask students to identify parts of a book, such as its title or page numbers.

- The **Concepts About Print (CAP) test** assesses a student's print awareness. The CAP test is administered one-on-one, typically at the beginning and middle of a student's kindergarten year. During the CAP test, the teacher asks a student questions about a book's print. The teacher records the student's responses to the questions asked on a standardized rubric. This helps to identify specific areas of weakness for each student in terms of print awareness. These areas can then be reinforced and retaught in future lessons.

Planned Observations

Marie Clay's **Observation Survey** can be beneficial in the assessment of a student's letter recognition and alphabetic principle knowledge. The Observation Survey includes six literacy tasks:

1. Letter Identification

2. Concepts about Print
3. Writing Vocabulary
4. Hearing and Recording Sounds in Words
5. Text Reading
6. Word Test

During such assessments, a student may be asked to identify a letter's name, its sound, rhyming pairs, isolated initial/final phonemes, blending of compound words/syllables, and word segments, or to add or delete phonemes in words. Similarly, teachers can say a letter and ask students to write that letter on a sheet of paper. The teacher records student responses. In this way, the teacher can identify the skills that have not yet been mastered by a single student, small group, or entire class. The teacher can then use any of the aforementioned strategies to reinforce those skills within individuals, small groups, or whole-class instruction.

Using Multimodal Techniques to Develop Alphabet Knowledge

Developing alphabet knowledge in young children is important for reading instruction. Experts recommend doing so by using multimodal techniques. There are four multimodal styles: visual, auditory, reading/writing, and kinesthetic (VARK). Read more below about each of these styles and how to use them to reinforce alphabet knowledge.

Visual
Visual learning involves using various types of images, including maps, graphs, artwork, photos, videos, and other objects to help students understand information. Reinforcing alphabet knowledge in young children with visual techniques can be fun. Watching alphabet lessons like those offered by *ABC Mouse* or *Sesame Street* is an option. Teachers can also bring in items that start with the letters being taught, like apples for the letter "A."

Auditory
Auditory learners absorb information through listening and conversing. Recitation exercises, alphabet songs, and rhymes work well when teaching the alphabet to these students.

Reading/Writing
Some students learn best through reading and writing text. They can take notes and commit what they have read to memory; they also tend to do well on written exams. These children will appreciate reading alphabet books and writing out the alphabet in uppercase and lowercase forms.

Kinesthetic
Kinesthetic learners like hands-on experience. They want to be immersed in what they're learning. Learning the alphabet has to be a much more involved experience for these children, so teachers want to make it fun. Teachers can utilize arts and crafts, like building letters out of playdough. Scrambling up alphabet blocks and having students put them in alphabetical order is another activity kinesthetic learners might enjoy. To get students up and moving, you can hide cutouts of letters around the classroom or outside for a scavenger hunt.

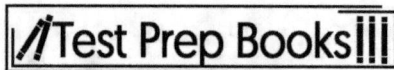

Predictable Texts

Predictable texts usually repeat phrases so that children can commit them to memory. They are best used with emergent readers, kindergarteners, and children that are struggling to learn how to read.

Predictable texts also make children aware of print concepts and alphabet knowledge. They learn what print looks and feels like on the pages of a book. They can see the spacing, font, and punctuation. They can see how illustrations are placed on the pages. Children can also learn how to properly hold a book. They make the connection between the letters on the pages and the words being read out loud. They begin to understand how those individual letters form words.

- Children also learn the following skills from predictable texts:
- Reading and speaking aloud
- Rhyming
- Articulation

Here are some popular predictable books:

- *Goodnight Moon* by Margaret Wise Brown
- *The Very Hungry Caterpillar* by Eric Carle
- *Brown Bear, Brown Bear, What Do You See?* by Bill Martin, Jr.
- *I Went Walking* by Sue Williams
- *Is Your Mama a Llama?* by Deborah Guarino

Predictable texts have their drawbacks, however. Because they rely heavily on repetition and images, children's decoding skills do not develop as well as they would with traditional reading lessons. Children are less inclined to learn more vocabulary words through predictable texts. This is why most experts suggest leaving these texts to younger or new readers.

Implications of Non-Alphabetic Languages for English Learners

Some written languages, like Chinese, are not alphabetic like English. Others, like German and Spanish, are much more phonetic than English. These factors affect literacy development in those learning English as a second language. Instructors should be prepared for students from a variety of backgrounds to enter their classrooms. Some of these students may have learning disabilities, and language barriers may make these disabilities hard to detect. Have as many tools as possible at your disposal to prepare yourself for the instruction and assessment of these students.

Someone that speaks an alphabetical, phonetically regular language, or a language that is spoken as it is written, may fare better when it comes to learning English reading skills. However, they may not pick up on the various contractions and inflections that are used in English. It is important to teach students words that can be made into contractions, like "will not" and "won't." Teachers can also use predictable texts to model and teach voice inflections.

English vowel sounds are also not found in many other languages. Non-English speakers may not be able to process them when hearing them in the classroom, and they will need special instruction to develop this skill. Spend time on the relationships between sounds, syllables, and letters.

Please also remember that some languages, like Arabic, are typically read left to right. So Arabic-speaking English learners will have to learn a new alphabet, new sounds, and a new reading direction.

Differentiating Instruction in Print Concepts, Alphabet Knowledge, and the Alphabetic Principle

It is important for teachers to tailor instruction to meet the various learning needs of their students through differentiated instruction. There are research-based ways that you can apply differentiation when teaching print concepts, alphabet knowledge, and the alphabetic principle.

When teaching these three areas, remember VARK. Teaching according to each of the VARK modalities will help teachers cover a majority of their students' needs. As a refresher, VARK refers to visual, auditory, reading/writing, and kinesthetic learning styles.

Print Concepts
Visual learners will appreciate learning print concepts from predictable books full of images, while auditory learners will appreciate hearing the patterned stories from those same books read aloud. Children who learn from reading and writing will enjoy independent reading assignments and writing exercises, like writing thank-you notes or letters. Kinesthetic students are active learners, so give them an activity like creating words with household items like macaroni noodles.

Alphabet Knowledge
Similar activities can be used to teach alphabet knowledge to different types of learners. Visual and kinesthetic learners may appreciate a letter jar; fill a clear jar with letter marbles and unmarked ones (beads and dice work as well). See if students can spot which letters are in the jar or, better yet, have them reach in and grab some and then announce which letters they've chosen. Instructors can simultaneously teach auditory and reading/writing learners the alphabet by reciting words like animal sounds and then asking the students to write down the letters that they think the sounds start with, like "M" for "moo." In fact, teachers could include many students in this game if they use photos or videos of animals making the sounds, and then ask the children to repeat the sounds and spell them.

Alphabetic Principle
Differentiation when teaching the alphabetic principle may be trickier because listening is so crucial; students with disabilities like dyslexia may struggle. If a disability is detected in a student, see that they get specialized help.

Children need to hear and see the difference between letters that are audibly similar, like "v" and "b." They also need to understand the difference between letters that are visually similar, like "p" and "q." Be sure to point out letter-sound relationships that do not make sense visually, like "gh." Use writing exercises, word cards, videos, and songs; these activities should cover most learning needs.

Many children enjoy word ladders, which are great exercises that help them build words with different patterns and sounds. Easy Teacher Worksheets offers free word ladders that teachers can use: https://www.easyteacherworksheets.com/langarts/1/wordladders.html.

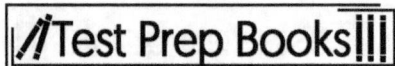

Domain II - Reading Development: Foundational Skills

Phonics and Other Word Identification Skills

Phonics Instruction

Phonics incorporates the alphabetic principle and decoding strategies. Phonics knowledge includes recognizing letter-sound correspondence. Students use phonics to sound out letter sequences and blend the sounds of the letter sequences together in order to form words.

Phonics instruction should begin with the decoding of simple syllable patterns. Upon mastery of simple patterns, more complex patterns can be introduced. The following characteristics are present in an effective phonics program:

1. The goal and purpose are clarified at the beginning of each lesson.

2. Visual and concrete material, such as letter cards and dry-erase boards, are used.

3. Direct instruction of letter sounds is provided through a series of mini lessons.

4. Direct instruction in the decoding of letter sounds found in words is provided, such as sounding out letters and blending sounds into words.

5. Students partake in guided and independent practice during which immediate feedback is provided. Activities such as word reading and word sorts, which incorporate previously taught spelling patterns, can reinforce explicit phonics instruction.

6. Effective phonics programs allow students to apply new phonics skills in a broad range of reading and writing contexts.

Phonics instruction stresses letter-sound correspondences and the manipulation of phonemes. Through phonics instruction, students discover the different sounds of a spoken language and how a written language's letters and symbols relate to one another. It is through the application of phonics principles that students are able to decode words. When a word is decoded, the letters that make up the printed word are translated into sounds. When students are able to recognize and manipulate letter-sound relationships of single-syllable words, then they are able to apply such relationships to decode more complex words. In this way, phonics aids reading fluency and reading comprehension.

Sight words, sometimes referred to as high-frequency words, are used often but may not follow the regular principles of phonics. Sight words may also be defined as words that students are able to recognize readily and read without having to sound them out. Students are encouraged to memorize words by sight so their reading fluency is not deterred through the frequent decoding of regularly occurring irregular words.

Word recognition occurs when students are able to recognize and read a word automatically and correctly. Phonics and sight word instruction help with the promotion of accurate and automatic word identification and recognition. Once students are able to readily identify and recognize words, then they can focus on the meaning of the text and development of reading comprehension skills.

Sequencing Phonics Instruction

Most children are taught systematic phonics, also known as sequencing. Children are taught the least to most difficult phonics concepts, beginning with letter-sound relationships, then vowel sounds, and finally syllabication. Systematic phonics is best taught to children in grades K–2, the years when they are building on emerging reading skills.

Decoding is using knowledge of phonics to recognize and pronounce printed words. Reading comprehension relies on decoding. Students need to be able to automatically recognize words when they read them; if they don't recognize the words, they need to use phonics to sound them out.

Once children are able to effectively decode, they can begin the process of encoding. Encoding is using phonics to write. Encoding is a valuable skill when learning syllabication and morphemic analysis. Exercises in which children learn to create words by combining different morphemes require encoding skills. If students are able to encode unfamiliar words, they may be able to automatically decode them the next time they come up.

Students need explicit phonics instruction and frequent opportunities to decode. As mentioned, these skills are the building blocks for literacy. Provide students with several activities so that they can practice these skills. Mastering phonics and decoding improves students' grammar, spelling, vocabulary, and oral and written communication.

Continuum of Phonics Skills

Sounding Out and Blending

Children must be able to sound out letters and blend each letter in decodable words. They must be able to blend syllables to create multisyllabic terms. They must be able to blend a variety of phonemes, including initial and final consonant blends, and they must be able to decode them. Along with blending, students should learn how segment phonemes into different words. The guidelines also stipulate that children are expected to decode words that contain digraphs and trigraphs.

Recognizing VC and CVC Words as Units

Students should be able to recognize vowel-consonant words (VC words) and consonant-vowel-consonant words (CVC words) as units. They must know how to use letter-sound relationships to interpret these words. Children must be able to spell VC and CVC words. They must demonstrate knowledge of vowel-consonant-e (VCe) syllables, one-syllable, and multisyllabic words. They must be able to decode words using VC and CVC word division patterns.

Decoding More Advanced Words

Students in grades K–5 should be able to decode increasingly complex letter combinations and phonics elements. They should know the vowel-vowel (VV) syllable division pattern and should have progressive knowledge of the ways that words are divided into syllables. They must be able to spell advanced words. They should have advanced knowledge of prefixes and suffixes.

Texas Gateway has phonics activity suggestions for K–5 teachers:
https://www.texasgateway.org/resource/target-2-lessons-support-phonics-grades-k-through-5.

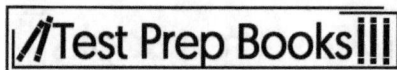

Delivering Explicit, Systematic Phonics Instruction

Research has shown that phonics and sight-word instruction is best accomplished using the following steps:

1. Phonics instruction should begin with **consonant sounds**. Consonant sounds block the flow of air through the mouth. Consonants can form either continuous or stop sounds. **Continuous sounds** are those that can be said for a long period of time, such as /mmm/. **Stop sounds** are said in short bursts, such as /t/.

2. Teach the following common and regular letter combinations:

   a. **Consonant digraphs:** Consonant digraphs are combinations of two or three consonants that work together to make a single sound. Examples of consonant digraphs are *sh*, *ch*, and *th*.

   b. **Consonant blends:** Consonant blends are sometimes referred to as **consonant clusters**. Consonant blends occur when two or three consonant sounds are blended together to make a single consonant sound. Unlike consonant digraphs, each letter in a consonant blend is identifiable. Examples of consonant blends are *gl, gr, pl, sm*, and *sp*.

   c. **Vowel digraphs:** Vowel digraphs are sets of two vowels that spell a single sound. A digraph is not a sound. Examples of vowel digraph pairs are *ow, ie, ae, ou, ei, ie*, and *oo*.

   d. **Diphthongs:** Diphthongs are the sounds created by letter/vowel combinations.

   e. **R- and l- controlled vowels:** These are words in which a vowel sound is controlled by an *r, l,* or *ll* following it. Examples include *car, girl, old*, or *call*.

3. Teach common inflected **morphological units**, which include word parts such as affixes or root words. Examples of morphological units that could be presented at this time are suffixes such as *-ed, -er, -est, -ing*, and *-s*.

4. Present common word patterns of increasing difficulty. **Word patterns** are made of sequences of vowels (V) and consonants (C). Examples include VC (*ear, egg, eat*, etc.), CVC (*cat, bat, map*, etc.), CCVC (*stop, frog, spot*, etc.), CVVC (*head, lead, dead*, etc.), and CVCe (*same, make, rake*, etc.).

5. Teach identification of vowel-consonant patterns and multisyllabic-word syllabication.

6. Discuss why some words are irregular, meaning that they are not decodable. Students may struggle decoding some words because the sounds of the letters found within the words do not follow predictable phonics patterns.

7. Time should be allotted for the instruction of common irregular sight words that are not readily decodable. However, this is usually not done until students are able to decode words that follow predictable phonic patterns at a rate of one letter-sound per second. Irregular sight words need to be gradually introduced. Words that are visually similar should not be shown in proximity to one another. The irregular words need to be practiced until students can read them with automaticity. New words are not introduced until the previous sets are mastered. The words are continuously reintroduced and reviewed thereafter.

8. When students first begin reading, they may be able to decode some words that have not yet been introduced to them merely by using letter-sound correspondences. The instruction of irregular words should be applied to these words as well.

Teaching Word Patterns

While reading has much to do with conceptual knowledge of English and awareness of the structures and rules of the language, recognizing word patterns can also help students see basic English principles. Being able to recognize familiar word patterns essentially helps students decode the pronunciation and even the meaning of unfamiliar words by recognizing core linguistic components.

The first step in identifying patterns is knowing how to sort words. When describing and searching for word patterns, sound is key. To begin, instructors can have students (or themselves) list single-syllable words that share similar beginnings, endings, or vowel sounds. For example, students can recognize that the *a* sound used in *bat* and *cat* is the same. Recognizing this sorting method provides insight on how to pronounce the words *that* or *fat*. Thus, students gain a tool for decoding words they haven't seen before.

Teachers should also examine words that are spelled differently but sound the same. For example, *veer*, *near*, and *tier* share a sound pattern but are spelled differently. This sheds light on how the vowels *ee*, *ea*, and *ie* sound between consonants. For an activity, students can group vowel combinations into columns that indicate a shared sound to help them recognize the connection between sound and spelling patterns. Another engaging activity would be to have students create small poems that use words with a specific sound. For example, using the vowel *i*, students can be encouraged to create a rhyme with three words, each with one syllable. The results should share common vowel and consonant sounds, such as *tip*, *ship*, and *dip* or *fig*, *lip*, and *skid*. Note how the vowel remains constant even while the consonants change.

Some single-syllable words, such as common sight words, have no clear pattern. The best way to teach these words (*the*, *to*, and others) is to have students visualize and learn them just as they are. One easy activity would be to play bingo or a similar visual game using single-syllable sight words to build familiarity with the everyday terms.

Sight Word Instruction

The goal of **sight word instruction** is to help students readily recognize regular and irregular high-frequency words in order to aid reading fluency and comprehension. Several factors affect the sequence of instruction for specific sight words. For example, before a child is exposed to sight words, he or she needs to be able to recognize and say the sound of all uppercase and lowercase letters. Students also need to be able to decode target words accurately before they recognize sight words. When irregular words are introduced, attention should be drawn to both the phonetically regular and the phonetically irregular portions of the words.

Before sight word instruction can begin, teachers need to identify high-frequency words that do and do not follow normal spelling conventions. Teachers may choose to select words that are used often within their students' reading materials, words that students have an interest in learning, or content-specific words. Alternatively, grade-level standardized sight word lists, such as the Dolch word lists, can be referenced.

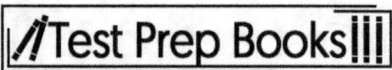

Domain II - Reading Development: Foundational Skills

Recognizing and Reading Sight Words

Repetition and exposure through guided and independent practice are essential in student retention of sight words. Each lesson should introduce only three to five new sight words and also review words from previous lessons. Visually similar words should not be introduced in proximity to one another. Sample activities through which sight words can be taught are listed below.

- Have students practice reading decodable texts and word lists.

- Teachers should read texts that contains the sight words that a class is currently learning. As a teacher reads aloud, they should pause, point to, and correctly pronounce the words. Instead of pointing to the words, teachers can underline or highlight the words as they appear.

- Use flashcards to practice sight word recognition.

- Play games such as Bingo, Go Fish, and Memory.

- As students learn new sight words, they can write them in a sight word "dictionary." Ask students to write a sentence using each sight word included within the dictionary.

Spelling Sight Words

The spelling of high-frequency words should be taught after students have been exposed to the words, can readily recognize the words, and can read the words. The following multisensory strategies can be used to help students master the spelling of high-frequency sight words.

- **Spell reading**: Spell reading begins when a student says the high-frequency word. Then, the student spells out the letters in the word. Lastly, the student reads the word again. Spell reading helps commit the word to a student's memory when done in repetition.

- **Air writing**: When air writing, a student uses their finger to write the letters of a word in the air.

- **Arm tapping**: During arm tapping, a student says the word, then spells the word aloud while tapping on their arm as they say each letter, and finishes by saying the word again.

- **Table writing**: Students write the word on the table. A substrate, where the word is written in sand or shaving cream, can be added to the table.

- **Letter magnet spelling**: Arranging letter magnets on a metal surface, such as a cookie sheet, is a fun way for students to learn how to spell sight words. Because this strategy is seen as a game to the student, letter magnet spelling increases student motivation to write words.

- **Material writing**: Students can use clay, play dough, Wikki sticks, or other materials to form letters that are used to spell the words.

Advanced Decoding and Orthographic Patterns

As students become more advanced in their decoding abilities, they will begin to read words that are increasingly more complex linguistically. Teachers should continue using decodable text so that students can continue practicing phonics elements and sight words that have already been taught.

Whole-to-part instruction can be used with students who display more advanced decoding abilities. During whole-to-part instruction, a sentence, a word, and then a sound-symbol relationship is the focus of instruction. Additionally, CVCC, CCVC, and CVVC words that contain common and regular letter combinations can be taught as well as regular CVCe words. Teachers can begin introducing less common phonics elements, such as *kn* or *ph*. It is during this stage that students are taught how to add common inflected endings or suffixes (*-ed, -er, -est, -ing,* etc.) to single-syllable base words.

Orthography is the study of a language's spelling conventions. Orthography includes the rules of spelling, hyphenation, capitalization, pronunciation, emphasis, and word breaks. Orthographic processing requires students to use their visual systems to envision, store, recall, and form words. The prescribed teaching sequence of orthographic patterns is found in chart on the following page.

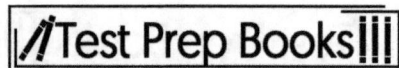

Orthographic Pattern	Example of Pattern
Awareness of letter-sound correspondences	Understanding that each letter has a certain sound as well as a name
Understanding that letters form words	Recoding certain CVC words like *dog*, *hug*, and *jar*
Simple consonant blends and matching sound patterns	Recognizing onsets and rimes of single-syllable words like *cat* as *c-at* and *star* as *st-ar*
Recognizing single-syllable words	Uses CVC, CCVC, or CVCC patterns
Ability to read more complex consonant blends	Reading and recognizing single-syllable words like *cross*, *lamp*, and *track*
Long versus short vowels	Identifying words that contain long and short vowel sounds
Vowel-Vowel and Vowel-Consonant Digraphs	Identifying words like *whey*, *tree*, and *phone*
Vowel-Vowel Digraphs that have the same sound	Identifying sounds such as /ay/, /ai/, or /a-e/
Vowel-Consonant Digraphs can be associated with different sounds	Identifying words like *cool* versus *boot*, *harm* versus *hare*, etc.
Complex single-syllable digraphs and trigraphs	Introducing the *tch* trigraph
Syllabication	Ability to split words into syllables
"Silent Letters" within words	Identifying words that contain silent letters such as *write*, *knock*, or *plumb*
Blending of two-syllable words	Reading two-syllable words such as *stumble*, *candle*, etc.
Morphemes within two-syllable words	Identifying correct syllabication of two-syllable words like *post-pone* versus *po-stpone*
Meaning of morphemes	An example would be knowing "macro" means "large" or "great"
Understanding letter clusters	Identifying that the "s" at the end of a word means it's plural, and that the "ed" at the end of a word means it's in past tense.
Syllabication of nonconventional morphemes with multisyllabic words	Syllabication of morphemes that are not pronounced how they are written, like *ance* or *tion*.

Homophones, Homographs, and Contractions

Students will need to know how to spell and decode common homophones, homographs, and contractions.

- Homophones: Terms that sound alike but are different in meaning and spelling.
- Homographs: Terms that are spelled alike but sound different and have different meanings.
- Contractions: Shortened versions of words that leave out letters.

Homophones and Homographs

When teaching homophones, remember that regional dialects may pronounce these words differently. Consider the homophones "aural" and "oral." The "au" part of "aural" may be pronounced "awe" in a different dialect. Look over a list of homophones to find other examples.

Context is everything when it comes to teaching homophones and homographs. Researchers suggest teaching pairs of these words separately in contexts where they make sense. If you present them together, it can be incredibly confusing for students.

Teach the spelling of homophones one at a time. According to experts, it makes sense to do so in alphabetical order. So, when teaching a pair of words like "fair" and "fare," you would teach "fair" first. Use "fair" in sentences and word games to enforce the students' knowledge of the word and help them decode it. Repeat this process with each homophone being taught.

Many teachers use sight-word cards to teach homophones. These cards usually have the word written out on one side and an image of the word on the other. These help children remember the word by making a visual connection to it. Books that contain images and large print are also great for this purpose. Children can point out words, sound them out, and infer what they mean from the surrounding text.

As mentioned previously, teaching homographs in context is also key. Defining the words when they are used in stories is always helpful, but using visuals to support that information is highly recommended. When teaching the noun form of a word like "building," show an image of an actual building. When teaching the verb form of the word "building," show pictures or videos of builders at work. This will help children grasp the difference between the two terms. Another technique would be to show pictures and ask the students to identify which version of the word is being demonstrated in the image.

Using riddles to teach homographs is another technique experts recommend. This approach can be used when teaching spelling. For example, giving the students a riddle with letters of the homographs missing can be fun. This way, students have to guess which letters are required to complete the words.

Other teachers also recommend teaching homographs in humorous ways. Teachers can do this by finding cartoons that use the homographs they're teaching and helping students recognize them.

Contractions

Educators often refer to contractions as shortcuts taken in written and verbal language. Enforce this concept when teaching them to students. There are several ways to do this. Naturally, the first step is ensuring that students can spell both the original and contracted form of words. Show the class which letters are to be crossed out and replaced with apostrophes, and then have some fun with it.

Letter tiles are great for teaching spelling and literacy. They are color-coded blocks that have letters and phonemes printed on them, so students can visualize the creation of words. Teachers can use physical and virtual versions. When teaching contractions, have students spell out the full version of words and then ask them to remove letters to create contractions, based on the cross-out lessons they previously learned. These colorful squares are great at keeping students' attention.

When teaching contractions, emphasize the importance of placing the apostrophe correctly. After students have omitted letters from the letter tiles, explain to them that the apostrophe must take the place of those letters.

Word strips are a fun way to teach spelling and apostrophe placement. Teachers can create them in a word processing program. As displayed in the image below, the full forms of each word in the contraction go on the left side of the strip, while the apostrophe and the letters that follow go on the right side. These can be demonstration tools, or an activity in which the students must figure out how to fold the strips and create the contractions.

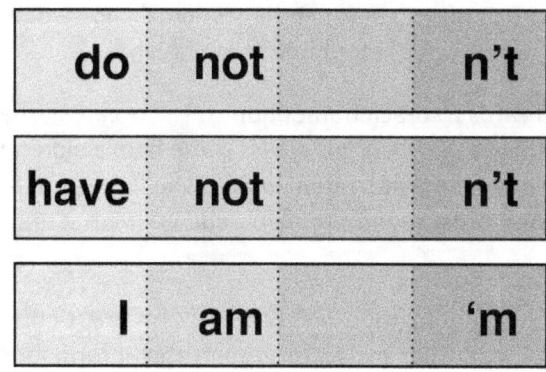

Self-Monitoring and Pre-Teaching Strategies

Children who are developing reading fluency and comprehension skills can become frustrated when presented with unfamiliar words in a given text. With direct phonics instruction, educators can teach children to decode words and then use context clues to define the words while reading. If children have a strong enough understanding of language structures, educators can ask them to consider what part of speech the unknown word might be and use that information to help infer its meaning. Focusing on visual clues, such as drawings and photographs, may help children decipher unknown words. They could also look for the word in another section of the text to see how it relates to the overall meaning. Competent readers **self-monitor**, meaning they listen to themselves as they read both to notice any discrepancies between the words they see and the sounds they say and to ensure that what they have read makes sense.

One of the most valuable strategies for helping children to understand new words in their reading is **pre-teaching**, in which teachers select the unfamiliar words in the text and introduce them to the class before reading. Educators using this method should be careful not to simply ask the children to read the text and then spell the new words correctly. They should also provide clear definitions and give children the opportunity to read these words in various sentences to decipher word meaning. This method can dramatically reduce how often children stop reading in order to reflect on unknown words. Educators are often unsure as to whether to correct every mispronounced word a child makes when reading. If the mispronounced word still makes sense, it is sometimes better to allow the child to continue to read, since the more the child stops, the more the child's reading comprehension and fluency are negatively affected.

Strategies for Reinforcing Development of Beginning Reading Skills

Sometimes students forget the concepts they were taught during the emergent reading stage. To reinforce their knowledge, instructors can use some popular research-based strategies, like close reading. Close reading, also known as rereading, is an integral strategy used to reinforce students' beginning reading skills. Research has shown that rereading improves students' analytical skills.

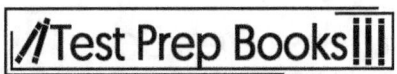

After reading a passage with students in class, ask them questions about the passage's key concepts. The questions cause the students to reread portions of the passage. Ask questions about the main character, the actions they took, and what students think certain words mean. Give the students highlighters so that they can highlight words that they don't understand; the instructor can clarify these.

See if students can make personal connections to the text. Are they reading about characters around their age? What do these characters look like, and what do they like to do for fun? It is important for children to see themselves represented in the books and other materials they're learning from. The more representation, the more likely they are to keep reading. Choose reading content that reflects the diversity of your classroom.

Some students are more shy than others, so reading out loud may not appeal to them. These students may feel discouraged from practicing reading. If a particular student is struggling, find a way to provide them with individual assistance. During individual sessions, define the terms the students are struggling with, and have them pronounce those terms out loud.

Teachers can also ask students to write a summary of the passage and its meaning. This not only forces them to reread, but it may also help them to display newly taught concepts in their writing, like their understanding of phonemes, homophones, homographs, and contractions. Their spelling skills will also be on display.

Supporting Different Types of Learners

The following strategies can be used to develop phonological and phonemic awareness in students who struggle with reading, disabled learners, special-needs students, English Language Learners (ELLs), speakers of nonstandard English, and advanced learners:

- Differentiated instruction for students with diverse literacy profiles should include the re-teaching and/or emphasis of key skills, such as blending and segmenting. Such instruction should be supported through the employment of a variety of concrete examples that explain a concept or task. Teaching strategies of such concepts or tasks should utilize visual, kinesthetic, and tactile modalities, and ample practice time should be allotted.

- Instruction of phonological and phonemic awareness can also be differentiated for ELs and speakers of nonstandard English. Most English phonemes are present in other languages. Therefore, teachers can capitalize on the transfer of relevant knowledge, skills, and phonemes from a student's primary language into the English language. In this way, extra attention and instructional emphasis can be applied toward phonemes and phoneme sequences that are nontransferable between the two languages.

- Advanced learners benefit from phonological and phonemic instruction with greater breadth and depth. Such instruction should occur at a faster pace and expand students' current skills.

Assessing Phonological and Phonemic Awareness

Entry-level assessments, progress monitoring, and summative assessments need to be administered in order to determine students' phonological and phonemic awareness. Appropriate formal and informal assessments for such purposes include:

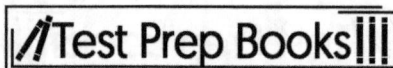

Domain II - Reading Development: Foundational Skills

The Yopp-Singer Test of Phonemic Segmentation
The **Yopp-Singer Test of Phonemic Segmentation** is an oral entry-level or summative assessment of phonemic awareness during which a teacher reads twenty-two words aloud one at a time to a single student. The student is to break each word apart by stating the word's sounds in the order that they are heard, and the teacher records the student's responses. Correctly segmented letter sounds are circled, and incorrect responses are noted. If a student does well, then he or she is likely to do well in other phonemic areas. Upon poor student performance, the sound(s) with which a student struggles should be emphasized and/or retaught shortly after the time of the assessment.

Recognizing Rhyme Assessment
Word awareness, specifically awareness of onset-rime, can be assessed as a progress-monitoring activity. During the **recognizing rhyme assessment**, the teacher says two words. Students are to point their thumbs up if the words rhyme and down if the words do not rhyme. Immediate feedback and remediation are provided if the majority of the students respond incorrectly to a word pair.

Isolation or Matching Games
Games can be used to identify initial, medial, and final phonemes. During a **phoneme-isolation activity**, the teacher says one word at a time. The student is to tell the teacher the first, medial, or last sound of the word. During **phoneme-matching activities**, a teacher reads a group of words. The student is to say which two words from the group begin or end with the same sound. A similar activity can be completed to assess deletion and/or substitution (e.g., "What word would result if we replaced the /c/ of *cat* with an *h*?"). In this way, teachers can assess if remediation or extra instruction on initial, medial, or final phonemes is required and develop lessons accordingly.

Phoneme Blending Assessment
In the **phoneme blending assessment**, a teacher distinctly says all the sounds within a word and then asks the student to say the word that they hear when the sounds are put together quickly. This skill will be needed when students learn letter-sound pairs and decipher unknown words in their reading. Thus, mastery of this assessment can be used as an indicator to the teacher that the students are ready to learn higher-level phonological and/or phonemic tasks.

Please note that student results should be recorded, analyzed, and used to determine if students demonstrate mastery over the assessed skill and/or identify the needs of students. If mastery is not demonstrated, then the assessments should be used to determine exactly which letter-sound combinations or other phonemes need to be remediated. Any of the strategies earlier addressed (rhyming, blending, segmenting, deleting, substituting) can be used for such purposes.

Syllabication and Morphemic Analysis Skills

Word Analysis

Phonics and decoding skills aid the analysis of new words. **Word analysis** is the ability to recognize the relationships between the spelling, syllabication, and pronunciation of new and/or unfamiliar words. Having a clear understanding of word structure, orthography, and the meaning of morphemes also aids in the analysis of new words.

However, not all words follow predictable patterns of phonics, morphology, or orthography. Such irregular words must be committed to memory and are called sight words.

Phonics skills, syllabic skills, structural analysis, word analysis, and memorization of sight words lead to word recognition automaticity. **Word recognition** is the ability to correctly and automatically recognize words in or out of context. Word recognition is a prerequisite for fluent reading and reading comprehension.

Structural and Syllabic Analysis

Structural analysis is a word recognition skill that focuses on the meaning of word parts, or morphemes, during the introduction of a new word. Therefore, the instruction of structural analysis focuses on the recognition and application of morphemes. **Morphemes** are word parts such as base words, prefixes, inflections, and suffixes. Students can use structural analysis skills to find familiar word parts within an unfamiliar word in order to decode the word and determine the definition of the new word. Identification and association of such word segments also aids the proper pronunciation and spelling of new multisyllabic words.

Similarly, learning to use phonics skills with more difficult words depends on a reader's ability to notice syllable structures within words that have more than one syllable. **Syllabic analysis**, or **syllabication**, is a skill that teaches students how to analyze words and separate them into syllables. **Syllables** are phonological units that contain a vowel sound. Teaching students how to break apart multisyllabic words into morphological and phonological units can greatly help them not to be intimidated by long words, since these tools will help them use syllable types to make longer words seem like a series of smaller words. The identified syllables can then be blended, pronounced, and/or written together as a single word. This helps students learn to decode and encode the longer words more accurately and efficiently with less anxiety. Thus, syllabic analysis leads to the rapid word recognition that is critical in reading fluency and comprehension.

The following table identifies the six basic syllable patterns that should be explicitly taught during syllabic instruction:

Basic Syllable Patterns		
Name of Syllable Type	Characteristics of Syllable Type	Examples
Closed	A syllable with a single vowel closed in by a consonant.	lab, bog, an
Open	A syllable that ends with a single vowel. Note that the letter *y* acts as a vowel.	go, me, sly
Vowel-Consonant-Silent *e*	A syllable with a single vowel followed by a consonant then *e*.	like, rake, note, obese
Vowel Teams	A syllable that has two consecutive vowels. Note that the letters *w* and *y* act as vowels.	meat, pertain, bay, toad, window
R-controlled	A syllable with one or two vowels followed by the letter *r*.	car, jar, fir, sir, collar, turmoil

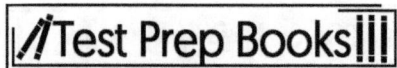

| Consonant *le (-al, -el)* Also called final stable | A syllable that has a consonant followed by the letters *le*, *al*, or *el*. | puddle, stable, uncle, bridal, pedal |
| Other final stable syllables | A syllable at the end of words can be taught as a recognizable unit such as *cious, age, ture, tion,* or *sion*. | pension, elation, puncture, stumpage, fictitious |

Teaching Syllabication and Morphemic Analysis

Syllabication occurs when words are broken down into syllables. The TEKS guidelines specify that students should use resources to develop their knowledge of syllabication to help improve their vocabularies. These resources can include virtual and print mediums.

Morphemic analysis involves dividing a word into parts in order to understand it. The TEKs for ELAR state that students should increasingly develop their knowledge of word structure via morphology. The guidelines go on to say that morphemic analysis is necessary for students' spelling, decoding, and overall communication skills.

Syllabication and morphemic analysis are part of phonological awareness. Children should start learning how to break words into parts as early as kindergarten.

When students are confronted with a word they do not understand and cannot pronounce, teachers can use the following syllabication exercise:

1. Write a multisyllabic word on the chalkboard or whiteboard.
2. Ask students to identify and count the vowels in the word.
3. Ask whether the vowels are together or if there are consonants between them.
4. Draw lines between the syllables in the word and ask students to count the syllables.
5. Point to each syllable, sound them out, and ask students to repeat.
6. Finally, tell the class to read all the syllables together to pronounce the word.

Morphemes can be taught similarly, except that teachers would draw lines between roots, prefixes, and suffixes. Children can use this strategy as they advance through grade six; however, by that grade, they should know how to look up words they do not understand online or in print dictionaries. There are many resources available that provide detailed explanations about the pronunciation and structures of words.

As students improve their syllabication and morphemic analysis skills, their communication skills will improve as well. According to the TEKS for ELAR, teachers should emphasize these two skills between kindergarten and sixth grade.

Compound Words

When two words are combined to create a new one, that new word is called a compound word. Educators can teach their students to decode and spell compound words in a variety of ways.

Letter blocks and tiles are great for teaching compound words. Create a word like *birthday* with the tiles or the blocks. Ask students to point out the two different words, and then separate them. Do this with more common compound words.

When your students are ready, present them with a word bank containing small words that can be used to create compound ones. This can be done in two ways. First, the students can pick out the words and write them together themselves. Second, they can be given a fill-in-the blank exercise in which one word is already provided.

Here is a fun visual exercise to teach children compound words. Provide them with two visual depictions of the meanings of two combinable words. See if they can figure out the compound word by recognizing the images and making the connection to the words. For example, show them a photo of a blue square and a photo of a berry. Ask what compound word is formed by combining the two shorter words.

The TEKS Guide, which is sponsored by the Texas Education Agency, recommends an even simpler exercise to test decoding skills. The TEKS Guide suggests having students read aloud from a provided list of compound words. Make a record of which words the students pronounce correctly, and then assess which words they need some help with.

With time, students should also develop stronger spelling skills. Conducting a spelling assessment after each compound word lesson will help students remember them, and it helps teachers see which words students need to study further.

Syllable Spelling Patterns

The methodology of grouping and recognizing patterns in single-syllable words can also apply to multisyllable words. However, because these words are more complex, the pattern scope must be broader. Teachers must reexamine similar-sounding vowel groups and consonant relationships as with singular-syllable words. It may also help to review the six syllable spelling patterns: open, closed, vowel team, silent vowel *e*, consonant *le*, and *r*-controlled patterns.

As a class activity, students can spend time grouping individual words into the spelling patterns to demonstrate their knowledge of English sounds and how the letters function in the words. The instructor should explain the categories, then name a word, have the students say it back, and finally group the word into its appropriate category. For example, the word *throat* has a kind of *oh* sound because of the vowel team *oa*. Instructors should also distinguish closed- and open-syllable spelling patterns. **Open** reflects a long vowel ending sound, such as *tiger*, with an exaggerated *-er* sounding ending; alternately, the **closed** pattern reflects a short vowel sound toward the end as seen in the word *darken*.

The **r-controlled vowels** are also important to highlight. Words such as *fur* and *car* stand out because of how the *r* sounds more prevalent than the vowel. To practice this, students can list words such as *cart*, *short*, *turtle*, and *fertile* on the board so they can have a visual reference, or the teacher can go around the class and have students name such words aloud. Again, it is important to hear the words and examine them visually in order for students to grasp how the words function and operate.

With multisyllable words, it is important to review consonant diagraphs and how they function. Because there are many diagraphs with different pronunciations, it is important to demonstrate how they differ

in various words, such as the *ch* in *Christmas* and *charity*. Students should also be able to compare how the placement of diagraphs alters pronunciations, such as with *anchor* or *pitch.*

When it comes to approaching multisyllable words in general, teachers should emphasize sounding out the words in order to grasp the pronunciation. Another good strategy for learning larger words is to have students break a word down by syllables and then combine them to complete the whole word. Again, an interactive approach to these principles will help students grasp the material more easily.

Types of Morphemes

There are many common morphemes in English, like -er, -ish, and -ful. You can find a comprehensive list of them online. There are different types, including roots, base words, inflections, and derivations.

Inflectional and derivational morphemes, in particular, are known as bound morphemes. Bound morphemes cannot stand on their own; they have no meaning unless they are connected to other bound morphemes, roots, or base words. Some examples are *-s*, *-ing*, and *-en*.

Inflectional morphemes showcase the grammatical purpose of a word. They help create comparative, possessive, singular, and plural words. They also help create the tense of words, like present or past.

When derivational morphemes are added to words, they change their grammatical identity. For example, adding -ly to the word *kind* transforms it into an adverb.

It doesn't hurt to give a refresher on commonly used morphemes. Review what they mean and quiz students on them. The more morphemes the students understand, the better they will become at decoding compound words.

Teaching Multisyllabic Words that Contain Two or More Morphemes

One method of teaching children multisyllabic words with two or more morphemes is to write a number of prefixes, roots, and suffixes on the board and ask students to practice creating as many words as they can. Teachers can give them specific assignments, like telling students to create words beginning with *re-* or ending with *-ly*. This activity will also help children with spelling.

To further reinforce their decoding and spelling skills, provide students with a writing activity. Whether it's a free writing session or a prompted one, give students a list of words with compound morphemes and ask them to write at least one paragraph using them.

For younger students, flip-and-find word cards are helpful for teaching compound morphemes. You can even purchase some blank ones so that you can write your own words on them. Preselect groups of two or three cards with morphemes on them. Raise one flap and provide a hint as to what is under the remaining flaps, and then ask students to guess which words might be there. These are just a few ways to help students develop knowledge of morphemes.

Chunking and Syllabication

Chunking—breaking down multisyllabic words into morphemes—is a technique many teachers use to teach students to read morphemes. Syllabication is a similar tactic. These methods will prepare children to read increasingly complex texts.

Syllabication helps students understand vowel sounds. Learning to do this helps students recognize the versatility of vowels, and it also helps them learn to spell words with specific vowel sounds properly. Syllabication and chunking are important techniques that helps children understand homophones and homographs.

Chunking is important to decoding. By breaking words down into chunks, children learn to identify the important parts of those words. Children are more likely to remember words that they broke down because they had to assess each part. Students are also better able to organize information when they learn chunking skills.

When students encounter words that they do not know, they will have the knowledge of syllabication and chunking to help them. If teachers have spent time teaching them the meanings of various morphemes and the sounds that various vowels make, they will be able to pronounce more words and build their vocabularies.

These two techniques can be taught during guided reading sessions. This will enable the teacher to learn which words are harder for their students to break down than others. Having the assistance of the teacher while learning this process is crucial. It is also imperative that students be given assignments to practice their newfound skills.

Less Common Syllable Types and Morphemes

As mentioned previously, the six types of syllables in the English language are closed, open, vowel team, vowel-consonant-e, vowel-r, and consonant-le. However, there are odd vowels that do not fit into these categories. These odd syllables include unstressed, schwa syllables.

Schwa syllables those in which the vowel makes neither its typical long or short sound; instead, it typically makes a short *u* sound. Some words that have the schwa syllable are b<u>a</u>lloon, <u>a</u>gain, and an<u>i</u>mal. Unstressed syllables are actually the most commonly used; they just are not taught as equally as the six most popular types.

Experienced educators recommend introducing the schwa when teaching multisyllabic words. Teaching schwas with similar sounds in groups is a method many teachers use. So, words like *again*, *about*, and *around* would be taught together.

Teach the relationship between stressed and unstressed syllables. An activity where students clap their hands when a stressed syllable is announced helps them recognize when it is used and when an unstressed syllable is coming up in a word. While doing this activity, students will inadvertently also learn how to spell these words—an added bonus!

Bound morphemes, also known as cranberry morphemes, have no meaning or grammatical function; however, they still help to distinguish words from one another. The name "cranberry morpheme" is a nod to the morpheme "cran," which has no meaning on its own. Other examples of cranberry morphemes are re<u>ceive</u>, in<u>fer</u>, and com<u>mit</u>. They are also known as leftover and blocked morphemes.

Teaching bound morphemes needn't be hard. Utilize word banks and flash cards to teach them. Provide students with one list of these morphemes and another of words they commonly go with. Then see how many students can accurately match them all.

Students will also need to learn multisyllabic words with multiple sound-spelling patterns, which are combinations of two or more letters that represent specific sounds. These sounds are grouped together to create words. Children can be taught these patterns while they are learning to read.

As an instructor, choose a book to read with your class. If students are young, use a patterned book. Read the words in the book out loud while pointing to them. Students should then be asked to point out words with certain sound-spelling patterns. This is especially effective in small groups. For larger classes, present a story on a projection screen and read along with the class that way. Write the patterns down as you go and put them up on the board later. Focus on teaching these patterns for the next few lessons.

Using Print and Digital Resources

The classroom is the perfect place to teach children that they can use digital resources along with print ones to enhance key literacy skills like pronunciation and word origins.

Digital Resources

Beyond using search engines to look up word meanings or pronunciations, there are other digital resources teachers can use. PowerPoint or other presentation software, virtual letter tiles, YouTube, Ted-Ed videos (https://ed.ted.com/), and collaborative online games are all examples of educational digital resources.

Many students have laptops or tablets that they can use to engage in virtual lessons. Syllabication, pronunciation, and other skills can be taught by creating interactive spelling and vocabulary lessons. They can be connected to games and puzzles that make students practice what they have learned. These resources should have sounds and images accompanied by text.

Use PowerPoint to project text and images onto a screen. Use the presentation tools to highlight, underline, circle, or animate content. Have students make their own PowerPoint presentations. Break them into groups of four or less and assign a word or two that they need to chunk, define, and describe the origin of in just a few slides.

When students are at a loss for how to sound out words on their own, there is an abundance of online resources, like Merriam's Learner's Dictionary and its pronunciation tool (https://www.learnersdictionary.com/pronex/pronex.htm). Students can simply type in a word they are unfamiliar with and the site will pronounce it for them. Show students how to bookmark this site on a browser as a reference tool.

Print Resources

Dictionaries and thesauruses are not the only print resources available to students; others include workbooks, word cards, print assessments, flipbooks, worksheets, notebooks, and other written activities performed in class. All of these resources are helpful for teaching students syllabication, pronunciation, and word meanings and origins.

Naturally, books are the first print resources most children learn to use. Teach them important parts of the book like the title page or table of contents (TOC). Explain that the TOC, in particular, is what they refer to when they want to read a certain section in a book.

Many books also have glossaries, usually in alphabetical order. The glossary can be used as a tool to help children learn to alphabetize words up to the third letter. Help children navigate the glossary to look for words in the texts they are reading and explain how to find it in alphabetical order. Give them words to look up and tell them to write down the definitions they find.

Scholastic News and *Highlights* are publications written for children. Preselect articles in them and ask the class to find them, using their knowledge of TOCs. Read the articles together before assigning articles to groups to read and summarize.

Differentiating Instruction in Syllabication and Morphemic Analysis

Accommodating the individual needs of students is an important part of teaching syllabication and morphemic analysis skills. The degrees to which students learn vary greatly, and some are learning English for the first time. Here are some ways that teachers can differentiate their instruction.

Visuals
Children appreciate visuals. The more images teachers use in their instruction, the better. For students that do not yet know certain words in English, it is helpful to show pictures that represent the words they're learning.

Using visual elements like flip cards can help teach syllabication and morphemes. With morphemes, especially, teachers can use cards that have images that depict root words. But pictures are not the only visual materials that can be used. Toys and videos should also be used to teach. There are videos for children that explain how to break down and pronounce words. Toys can be used to show the actions that the words represent.

Interaction
Interactive activities like singing and marching to the beat of syllables and morphemes help engage students, especially auditory and kinesthetic learners. Group reading assignments where each child takes a turn reading out loud help with pronunciation. Creating poetry together is another way to enforce knowledge of syllables and morphemes.

Writing
Writing exercises help some children remember words more efficiently. Writing out how they think words should sound is an exercise that helps many learners.

There are a variety of helpful worksheets available that include diagramming syllables, chunking morphemes, and reviewing vocabulary words. Children that read more fluently tend to be better at writing activities than others.

Reading Fluency

Assessing Reading Fluency

Assessments are useful for identifying which students may be struggling with certain criteria as well as the specific areas of difficulty. Assessments can also indicate how well the material is being presented or provide vital clues on how to modify an individual student's instruction to help them grasp the content better. Generally, two types of assessments are used: informal and formal.

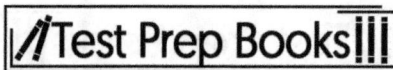

Informal assessments are not planned and lack a typical format or timeline. They can be as simple as watching and listening to how the students respond to answers in class or perform classwork. Observation is key. The instructor should perceive how students respond to reading and language concepts as well as how they interpret them. If a student is not understanding something such as a cultural reading concept, it may indicate that a more in-depth explanation is required. This will help the teacher adapt the instruction to enable the student to self-correct their own performance.

Formal assessments are partially based on observation but are planned and implemented with the design to see how students respond to specific stimuli. They give a clearer indication of students' strengths and weaknesses regarding the material. There are two primary methods for conducting formal assessments. The most conventional is a simple pencil-and-paper test in which students read prewritten questions and respond to them in writing. These physical answers provide a direct window into what the students know and how their reading comprehension is progressing. **Performance assessments** are a little less concrete but can provide a lot of insight into the student's mindset and reactions that are more three-dimensional than written assessments. This method does not use written responses, but instead analyzes students' performance in response to reading questions or activities. When giving performance assessments, it is important to bear in mind key questions: Does the student understand what they just read? Did they seem uncomfortable when presenting their answer? How accurate was their response? From here, new teaching strategies can be implemented, or the instructor can identify ways to provide specialized assistance to boost students' skills.

Differentiating Instruction in Reading Fluency

Instructors retrieve data from both informal and formal assessments. This data, whether written or gained through observation, is highly valuable in determining the effectiveness of teaching methods. Data-driven instruction guides reading improvement for all students simply because the data provides clear indications of where students are facing reading challenges or demonstrating strengths.

Differentiated instruction acknowledges that, while a group of students may be learning the same subject, the way each student learns and processes the subject is different. Differentiation involves looking at the different learning methods and reading areas and identifying which ones students respond to. Educators can then tailor, or differentiate, lessons to build on these skills and expedite the learning process. Differentiated instruction is divided into interest-based and ability-based instruction.

Much of a student's performance is based on their interest in the subject at hand. Sometimes a student may show difficulty reading because he or she is not engaged in the material. One way to encourage reading growth is to allow students to choose their learning activities. This will give students ownership over their own education, enabling them to have fun and to use specific activities that help them improve their reading abilities. For example, students more interested in visual activities may find reading more beneficial than listening to oral reading exercises.

Ability-based differentiation focuses on three core areas that determine reading proficiency and build skill. The first area of focus examines students' conceptual understanding of reading. If a teacher uses vocabulary or reading comprehension exercises in class, they will be able to examine how students are performing and modify instruction to address any confusion. This can also indicate students' preferences as well. The second differentiation looks at how students analyze and use the reading. Instructors must look at how students respond to questions and whether their interpretation is accurate. The final differentiation looks at how students evaluate and perform reading, creating a reaction that responds to the reading. The third differentiation looks at interpretation with the added step of using this knowledge to write or say something without being prompted. Identifying issues in one of these areas will narrow down where more emphasis must be placed to improve reading skills. Each reading area will affect the other two; improving one differentiated area will impact the others.

Continuum of Fluency Development

According to the TEKS for ELAR, students should be able to fluently read and comprehend text at their appropriate grade levels. Students' fluency levels should increase with each grade, from automatic letter naming to reading increasingly complex text.

When building fluency, students should be able to accurately and automatically name letters. Rapid automatic naming (RAN) is a process that reading teachers use to assess how quickly students can recall letters and words from memory. RAN has proven itself to be effective for word reading and predicting students' reading comprehension levels.

Fluency refers to the speed and accuracy with which students recognize words. Advanced readers will have no issue reading connected text (sentences that relate to each other). They can get practice doing this by reading along in class.

As children advance in grade level, they will read increasingly complex connected texts. Being able to comprehend how sentences relate to each other is important for reading chapter books, articles, and textbooks. At every grade level, students will be assigned classwork and homework that involves independent reading.

Students need to be able to keep up with what is being taught in class, and they need to be able to write coherent sentences. This all starts with reading fluency skills.

Key Concepts Related to Reading Fluency

Several factors influence a student's reading development skills. Students learn to read at varying ages. A student's background knowledge, first language acquisition, and family involvement in reading all affect a student's progress. Therefore, when to introduce fluency instruction cannot be determined merely by a student's age or grade level. Fluency instruction begins when a student can use basic decoding skills and can read 90 percent of connected text with accuracy. Routinely assessing a student's decoding and accuracy skills will help determine when to begin fluency instruction.

Even if students do not yet display automaticity, modeling can be used as an initial introduction to fluency. Modeling demonstrates social norms of reading rate and prosody while building vocabulary, academic language, and background knowledge.

Practice, Guidance, and Feedback

Accuracy and reading rate are fundamental components of fluency, but it is important to remember that practice is an essential component of effective fluency instruction. A student's accuracy and rate will likely increase if a teacher provides for them opportunities to learn words and use word-analysis skills.

Oral reading accompanied by guidance and feedback from teachers, peers, and/or parents has been shown to improve fluency significantly. In order to be beneficial, such feedback needs to provide targeted and differentiated advice on areas where a student needs improvement.

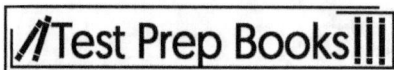

Domain II - Reading Development: Foundational Skills

Research-Based, Systematic, Explicit Strategies That Improve Fluency and Accuracy

Word-reading accuracy requires that students have a strong understanding of letter-sound correspondence and the ability to blend the sounds together accurately. Providing systematic, explicit instruction in phonemic awareness, phonics, and decoding skills will cultivate such accuracy. When students are readily able to identify high-frequency sight words, their accuracy improves. Therefore, instructors should provide ample opportunities to practice these words.

Strategies that Improve Fluency and Prosody

Reading aloud not only improves rate but also encourages appropriate expression, or **prosody**. When the teacher, the student, or an entire student body reads aloud, students become more exposed to the use of prosody; therefore, their reading expression is strengthened. When teachers read aloud, they model prosody, which cues students to the social norms of pace, pauses, inflection, emotion, and tone when reading different types of text. In **choral reading**, all students in the class read a passage aloud together, which allows them to hear text being read accurately and with good pacing and phrasing. By having students listen to recordings of themselves reading, teachers promote independent judgment and goal setting.

Reading theaters also support prosody. During reading theater instruction, students are assigned a character in a play. The emphasis is reading aloud with a purpose. Students use prosody to share their interpretations and understandings of their assigned characters' personalities and roles.

Phrase-cued reading is a third strategy that aids the development of prosody. During phrase-cued reading, teachers read a text aloud and mark where they pause or show intonation, emphasis, tone, inflections, and/or expression.

Addressing Common Factors that Disrupt Reading Fluency

How to Address a Range of Needs

Several strategies can be implemented to assist English Learners, speakers of nonstandard English, advanced learners, and readers who have diverse literacy profiles. However, it is always important to provide each student with reading materials and strategies that are appropriate for their specific reading level and area of concern.

Students with diverse literacy profiles benefit from direct instruction and feedback that teaches decoding and analysis of unknown words, automaticity in key sight words, and correct expression and phrasing. These learners also benefit from oral support. This may be provided through scaffolded reading, choral reading, partner reading, books on tape, and computer programs. Teachers should consistently offer opportunities for students to practice repeated reading and should gradually introduce more challenging reading levels as students progress.

Providing ample opportunities to read orally with a scaffolding approach, which gradually increases the difficulty of the work and slowly asks for more independence from the student, also helps this group. For instance, teachers may read a short passage and have students immediately read it back to them. Direct instruction in English intonation patterns, syntax, and punctuation are effective tools in assisting English language learners with the development of prosody.

In order to broaden and enhance fluency for advanced learners, teachers should gradually introduce more advanced texts across several content areas.

Continued Assessment of Student Fluency

Assessment of fluency must include entry-level assessments, progress monitoring, and summative assessments of accuracy, rate, and prosody. The results should be analyzed and interpreted in order to adjust instruction and provide struggling readers with proper interventions. Regular assessments also help teachers construct differentiated instruction in order to address the fluency needs of advanced learners.

Running records, widely used fluency assessments, allow teachers to document error patterns in reading accuracy as students read benchmark books. As the student reads aloud, the teacher holds a copy of the same text and records any omissions, mispronunciations, and substitutions. With this information, teachers can determine which fluency strategies a student does or does not employ.

Strategies for Promoting Reading Rate and Automaticity to Enhance Fluency

Reading aloud has proven effective in strengthening reading fluency. Whisper-reading accompanied by teacher monitoring has also proven effective for students who do not yet display automaticity in their decoding skills. Timed reading of sight phrases or stories also improves fluency with respect to rate. During a **timed-reading** exercise, the number of words read in a given amount of time is recorded. Routinely administering timed readings and displaying the results in graphs and charts has been shown to increase student motivation.

Timed-repeated readings, where a student reads and re-reads familiar texts in a given time, is a commonly used instructional strategy to increase reading speed, accuracy, and comprehension. Students read and re-read the passage until they reach their target rate.

Assessing Prosody

In order to assess prosody, a teacher listens for inflection, expression, and pauses as the student reads a connected text aloud. The Integrate Reading Performance Record Oral Reading Fluency Scale designed by the National Assessment of Educational Progress (NAEP) is also used to assess prosody. Students at levels 3 and 4 are considered fluent in prosody, while students at levels 1 and 2 are considered to be non-fluent.

Level 4: Reads mainly in large phrase groups. The structure of the story is intact, and the author's syntax is consistent, even if there are some deviations from the text. Most of the story is read with expression.

Level 3: Reads mainly in three- or four-word phrase groups. Majority of phrasing is appropriate and preserves syntax of the author. Little expression is present with interpreting the text.

Level 2: Reads two-word phrases with some three- or four-word groupings. Word-by-word reading may occur. Some word groupings may seem awkward, indicating that the student is not paying attention to the larger context.

Level 1: Reads word-by-word. Some occasional two-or-three-word phrases may be present, but they are not frequent, or they do not preserve meaningful syntax.

Assessing Reading Rate and Accuracy

Assessment of reading rate often begins with sight-word reading automaticity. Automaticity assessment may also include the decoding of non-words in order to determine if a student is able to decode words using sound-syllable correspondence.

Among the most commonly used measurements of reading rate is oral contextual timed reading. During a **timed reading**, the number of errors made within a given amount of time is recorded. This data can be used to identify if a student's rate is improving and if reading rate falls within the recommended fluency rates for the student's grade level. If a student's reading rate is below average, any of the previously identified research-based, systematic, explicit strategies that improve fluency with respect to rate may be applied.

One common timed assessment for reading accuracy is the **WCPM**, the words-correct-per-minute assessment. The teacher presents an unfamiliar text to a student and asks the student to read aloud for one minute. As the student reads, the teacher records any omissions, mispronunciations, or substitutions. These errors are subtracted by the total number of words in the text to determine a score, which is then compared to oral reading fluency norms. With this assessment, teachers can select the appropriate level of text for each student.

Recommended Reading Fluency Rates		
Grade	Semester	Correct Words Per Minute
First Grade	Winter	38
	Spring	40–60
Second Grade	Fall	55
	Winter	73–79
	Spring	81–93
Third Grade	Fall	79
	Winter	83–92
	Spring	100–115
Fourth Grade	Fall	91–99
	Winter	98–113
	Spring	106–119
Fifth Grade	Fall	105
	Winter	109–118
	Spring	118–128

Differentiating Instruction in Reading Fluency

What children read matters. Slowly moving them from story books to essays and textbooks is important; they need to be able to decode texts that are increasingly more difficult. As you are aware, each student will have different needs and skill sets when learning to read. Differentiating instruction in reading fluency is central to the learning environment. The following are a few well-researched suggestions.

Choice Boards

To assess comprehension on independent reading assignments, give students a few activity options. Write different activities on separate boards and ask them to select a few to complete. Organize the activities by learning preferences; for example, one board would contain activities that a visual learner would prefer, and another board would have some for auditory learners, and so forth. Students cannot pick more than one option from a particular board.

Interest Groups
Present students with some topics of interest, like sports, gaming, or music and provide books and magazines related to each. Let students pick one interest from those provided, and placed the students in groups based on their choices. Give each group its materials and instruct the students to read them and come up with a short report or presentation on what they have learned together. This is an excellent team-building exercise.

Tiered Assignments
With this technique, students will all be taught the same reading lesson, but they will be given different assignments based on skill level and learning preference. Before getting started, teachers should already know their students' reading levels.

After reading a text together in class, provide different levels of assignments to each student, such as reciting the most important parts of the story, drawing story maps, or reenacting the plot with puppets. The teacher's goal is to help teach the maximum number of students with the most effective techniques.

Practice Questions

1. Which of the following statements is true regarding decoding and encoding?
    a. Decoding is the spelling of words.
    b. Encoding helps students to recognize and read words quickly.
    c. Encoding is the application of letter-sound correspondences, letter patterns, and other phonics relationships.
    d. Decoding and encoding are learned in opposite stages or steps.

2. Kimberly draws a picture of her family, and her instructor asks her to write what she drew on the line below the picture. She puts together a jumble of letter-like forms rather than a series of discrete letters. The instructor asks her what she wrote, and she replies, "My family." Which stage of spelling development is Kimberly in?
    a. Pre-phonetic stage
    b. Semiphonetic stage
    c. Phonetic stage
    d. Conventional stage

3. Which of the following is true of word walls?
    a. Their primary purpose is to teach morphemes.
    b. They help students sort words they know, want to know, and have learned.
    c. They are primarily useful in the transitional phase of spelling.
    d. They group words that share common consonant-vowel patterns or letter clusters.

4. Which of the following displays a correct matching of an orthographic pattern with an example of that pattern?
    a. Vowel-vowel digraph that have the same sound: loud and wow
    b. Vowel-vowel digraph that have the same sound: read and speed
    c. Vowel-consonant digraphs with different sounds: stand and stair
    d. Vowel-consonant digraphs with different sounds: harm and have

5. A local newspaper is looking for writers for a student column. A student would like to submit his article to the newspaper, but he isn't sure how to format his article according to journalistic standards. What resource should he use?
    a. A thesaurus
    b. A dictionary
    c. A style guide
    d. A grammar book

See answers on the next page.

Answer Explanations

1. D: Choice *D* is correct because decoding and encoding are reciprocal phonological skills, meaning that the steps to each are opposite of one another. It is because of this reciprocal relationship that the development of phonics, vocabulary, and spelling are interrelated. The other answer choices are incorrect because they ascribe the wrong description to the given term.

2. A: Kimberly is in the pre-phonetic stage of spelling because she formed a jumble of letter-like forms rather than a series of discrete letters. This indicates that she only has precommunicative writing ability. Her letter-sound correspondence is limited. In the semiphonetic stage, she would have demonstrated a better understanding of the fact that letters represent sounds. She may have missed syllables in her words or used single letters to represent entire words, but she would have demonstrated letter formation and the alphabetic principle. The other choices list stages in which her spelling would be even further advanced.

3. D: Word walls are great tools for students as they learn to read, spell, and write. They help students learn unfamiliar words by visually grouping similar ones. Choice *A* is incorrect because the primary purpose of word walls is to provide visual groupings of words with similar letter patterns. Choice *B* is incorrect because it describes KWL charts typically used for reading. Choice *C* is incorrect because word walls are primarily useful in the phonetic stage.

4. B: Choice *B* is a correct match between *read* and *speed*. These two words are vowel-constant digraphs that have the same sound.

5. C: A style guide offers advice about proper formatting, punctuation, and usage when writing for a specific field, such as journalism or scientific research. The other resources would not offer similar information. A dictionary is useful for looking up definitions; a thesaurus is useful for looking up synonyms and antonyms. A grammar book is useful for looking up specific grammar topics. Thus, Choices *A*, *B*, and *D* are incorrect.

Domain III - Reading Development: Comprehension

Vocabulary Development

Assessing Development of Vocabulary Knowledge

The depth of a child's vocabulary knowledge directly correlates with their reading skills. The vocabulary they learn and how they learn it from pre-K on up matters. Children's knowledge of terms will be tested inside and outside of the classroom. The following are a few proven ways to assess students' vocabularies.

The most popular way to see which terms students know is to give them a vocabulary test. After teaching students a list of terms for a period of time, it is common for teachers to issue a multiple-choice or written test. With multiple-choice vocabulary tests, you prepare a word bank and then list the definitions of the words in no particular order. You can organize the words or the definitions by assigning them letters or numbers and then have the students match the correct number or letter to the corresponding definition or term.

For a more advanced test, you can give the students a worksheet with terms on it and provide a space for them to write in the definitions themselves. Use words that were featured in texts read in class to see if students understood their meanings.

Teachers can also test students' knowledge of antonyms and synonyms. They can compile a list of terms and either read them aloud and ask the class to name synonyms or antonyms, or they could give them a multiple-choice or written test similar to the ones described previously. This is a great way to see if the class gets the gist of terms that come up in their reading assignments.

The **Vocabulary Recognition Task (VRT)** assesses students' ability to recognize terms associated with a specific topic. In reading classes, educators can provide the students with a word bank and then ask them to circle words associated with the subject they have been reading about. The educator then grades the assignment based on the number of words circled correctly.

Vocabulary in Informational Texts

Vocabulary used throughout informational texts is generally quite different than vocabulary found in fictional print. For this reason, it is imperative that educators help children strengthen and increase their vocabulary inventory so that they can eventually become successful at reading and understanding informational text.

For instance, educators can point out *signal words* throughout texts to help children more readily and accurately identify the author's purpose. Authors employ specific vocabulary that spotlight their intent. For instance, if authors wish to list examples to support a main idea, they may use vocabulary such as *for example*, *such as*, or *as illustrated*. When displaying the chronological order of events, authors may use *first*, *lastly*, *before*, and *finally*. Some common compare and contrast vocabulary words include *but*, *same as*, *similar to*, *as opposed to*, and *however*. There are several key phrases that signal cause and effect relationships, including *because of*, *as a result of*, and *in order to*.

By using word walls and personal dictionaries, sorting vocabulary words according to theme, introducing text maps, and teaching children to become familiar with sidebars and glossaries in informational texts, educators will help expand their students' vocabularies and strengthen their abilities to read and comprehend informational texts successfully.

Vocabulary, Oral Language Development, Reading Comprehension, and Self-Sustained Reading

Vocabulary and oral language development are essential to each other. Most children start developing their vocabularies via speech and listening. The more terms they learn, the more they repeat. However, the bulk of our vocabulary comes from reading. Reading to and with children improves their language skills and broadens their vocabularies, which subsequently leads to better reading comprehension.

Children with strong reading comprehension are more likely to read independently for enjoyment. This is referred to as **self-sustained reading**. Children who often engage in self-sustained reading usually have a vast understanding of terminology. They also perform better in their reading classes and other subjects.

Students who love reading tend to have a thirst for knowledge and excel in the classroom. The more they learn, the more they are exposed to new jargon. This, in turn, expands their vocabularies and enables them to speak with many people about a multitude of topics. They may be more inclined to speak up in class or explain concepts to other students. Without a basic understanding of vocabulary, a child will lag in language, reading, and overall academic development.

TEKS for ELAR Guidelines for Vocabulary Development

The TEKS for ELAR provide requirements for helping students in kindergarten through grade 6 with their vocabulary development. Here is some of the advice as laid out in chapter 110.

- Texts should grow more challenging over the course of the school year to improve vocabulary.

- Students should be exposed to a variety of literature to help grow their vocabularies. Along the way, they should be learning basic sentence structure and grammar.

- Special attention should be given to **English language learners (ELLs)**, or students for whom English is a second language.

- These students are exposed to grammar in multiple languages, which can either put them at an advantage or disadvantage. Incorporate elements from their native languages to help them engage in decoding exercises and discourse.

- Employ different word-learning strategies to help students of varying abilities increase their vocabularies.

- Use flash cards, pop quizzes, or visual images so that children can associate words with certain images or actions. They should learn how to look up terms in dictionaries, thesauruses, and web search engines.

The TEKS for ELAR go on to describe the importance of frequent exposure to new vocabulary. Repeated exposure increases students' comprehension levels and response skills. This will prompt clearer

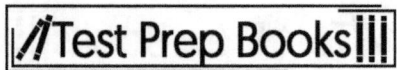

Domain III - Reading Development: Comprehension

communication with adults and their peers. They will also learn various nuances of language, such as inflection.

The guidelines frequently mention integrating the seven strands of knowledge into lesson plans. Doing so will make students more proficient learners, especially when it comes to language arts. Ultimately, children in kindergarten through grade 6 should feel confident enough to work on their self-sustained reading. Regular instruction focused on vocabulary development will meet the TEKS guidelines for ELAR as well as help children become better students.

Factors that Affect Vocabulary Development

The same factors that affect children's ability to learn in a class environment affect their vocabulary development. Cultural, socioeconomic, and language barriers should be considered when working with children of all ages.

In some cultures, people learn to read right to left versus left to right, as is the custom with most English speakers. Learning to read in a different language and adjusting to new cultural norms are actually assets. Because these students build translation skills as they learn, they often develop in-depth vocabularies.

Socioeconomic status also has an effect on children's vocabularies and reading development. Children from lower-income families tend to know fewer vocabulary terms and learn to read at slower rates than children from more affluent backgrounds. Family guardians who lack higher education may not engage with their children through regular reading activities. Lower-income families are also less likely to send their children to early education programs, such as daycare or pre-K; in this case, the children receive even less exposure to new words.

Although children learn a significant number of words through speech, they learn even more through frequent and wide reading. Wide reading is independent reading with everyday items, such as magazines, websites, or news articles. Both frequent and wide reading studies suggest that people, especially children, should read every day. The theory of wide reading actually recommends 2 hours of reading per day. The bottom line is, the more someone reads, the more intelligent they tend to be. This directly correlates with how well their vocabularies develop. Children who read frequently exhibit higher levels of concentration, sharper memories, and less stress. As a reading instructor, your job is to engage your students in regular reading assignments and assess how many words they have learned. You should also encourage them to read at home both independently and with family members.

Tiers of Vocabulary

There are three tiers of vocabulary:

Tier 1 is composed of basic vocabulary words that appear often in everyday speech (for example, "cat," "run," "almost"). Teachers do not usually need to teach these words, as children know them before entering grade school. Because they are so familiar, they make excellent words for new readers.

Tier 2 features words that occur fairly often in English but are more complicated than Tier 1 words or have multiple meanings. For example, "profitable," "eager," and "execute" are all Tier 2 words.

This is the level of vocabulary in which students progress furthest during their education, and it is often used to measure student progress.

Tier 3 includes words that appear only in specialized contexts. Students typically learn these words in context; for example, students learn "heterozygous" in biology class and "Industrial Revolution" in history.

There are also two types of vocabulary knowledge:

- **Recognition** refers to a student's ability to understand a word. For example, a student who understands the word "heinous" when it appears but would be unable to think of the word without reading or hearing it demonstrates recognition.

- **Production** is the capacity to use the word properly without reading or hearing it. A student who can use the word "aptitude" correctly without being prompted is said to be *producing* the word. Production necessitates a deeper level of vocabulary knowledge than recognition, as the student must remember the word well enough to think of it by themselves.

Selecting Words for Explicit Word Study

Choosing the right words to teach your students is important. The right words can help close the education gap between underachieving and advanced readers. **Explicit word study** intentionally focuses on specific words. Students will gain a full understanding of what these words mean and how to put them in the right context. Explicit vocabulary instruction is a cross-disciplinary method; it doesn't just apply to reading courses.

When selecting which words to teach, remember that there are three tiers of vocabulary instruction: (1) basic, (2) high frequency, and (3) low frequency. For the purposes of this guide, we will focus on tiers 2 and 3.

Tier 2
Tier 2 words transcend disciplines and situations; they are used in everyday conversation, academia, standardized tests, and literature. Some of these words have multiple definitions. Tier 2 terms might be the most important for students to learn because of their frequent appearance. When children use them, it showcases where they are in their education and signifies maturity. Some examples of these words are *evaluate, manipulate, maintain,* and *principle*.

Tier 3
Tier 3 words are low-frequency words and are field- or discipline-specific. These terms are taught to make students experts in particular subjects. They learn when to use these terms within their specified context. Some examples of tier 3 words are *lava, economics, integer,* and *hyperbole*.

Some strategies for teaching tier 2 and 3 words include class recitation, word searches and crossword puzzles, and making diagrams such as word trees. A word such as *chromosome* can be drawn; having students draw pictures of what they think words look like is an effective technique. You could also show them existing pictures when going over vocabulary in class. Assigning a visual to a word helps children remember what it means.

To make a word tree, give students a list of words. On the blackboard, write one word and draw branches. Have students call out which related words should go on those branches. This is especially effective when teaching suffixes and affixes.

Teach words according to their semantic word groups. The more a student becomes familiar with the frame of reference for terms, the easier they will remember them.

Vocabulary, Morphology, Semantics, Syntax, and Pragmatics

Vocabulary

Vocabulary consists of the bank of words that children can understand and apply fluently in order to communicate effectively. A strong vocabulary and word recognition base enables children to access prior knowledge and experiences in order to make connections in written texts. A strong vocabulary also allows children to express ideas, learn new concepts, and decode the meanings of unfamiliar words by using context clues. Conversely, if a child's vocabulary knowledge is limited and does not steadily increase, reading comprehension will be negatively affected. If children become frustrated with their lack of understanding of written texts, they will likely choose only to read texts at their comfort level or refuse to read altogether. With direct instruction, educators introduce specific words to pre-teach before reading, or examine word roots, prefixes, and suffixes. Through indirect instruction, educators ensure that students are regularly exposed to new words. This engages students in high-quality conversations and social interactions and provides access to a wide variety of challenging and enjoyable reading material.

Morphology

Morphology is the study of the structure and formation of words. A **phoneme** is the smallest unit of sound that does not necessarily carry meaning. Essentially, phonemes are combined to form words, and words are combined to form sentences. Morphology looks at the smallest meaningful part of a word, known as a **morpheme**. In contrast to a phoneme, a morpheme must carry a sound and a meaning. Free morphemes are those that can stand alone, carrying both sound and meaning, as in the following words: *girl, boy, man*, and *lady*. Just as the name suggests, **bound morphemes** are bound to other morphemes in order to carry meaning. Examples of bound morphemes include: *ish, ness, ly*, and *dis*.

Semantics

Semantics is the branch of linguistics that studies the meanings of words. Morphemes, words, phrases, and sentences all carry distinct meanings. The way these individual parts are arranged can have a significant effect on meaning. In order to construct language, children must be able to use semantics to arrange and rearrange words to achieve the particular meaning they are striving for. Activities that teach semantics revolve around teaching the arrangement of word parts (morphology) and root words, and then the teaching of vocabulary. Moving from vocabulary words into studying sentences and sentence structure leads children to learn how to use context clues to determine meaning and to understand anomalies such as metaphors, idioms, and allusions.

There are five types of semantic relationships that are critical to understand:

Hyponyms refer to more-specific words that fall into the same category as a more general word (e.g., mare, stallion, foal, Appaloosa, and Clydesdale are all hyponyms of horse).

Meronyms refer to a relationship between words where a whole word has multiple parts (meronyms) that comprise it (e.g., horse: tail, mane, hooves, ears).

Synonyms refer to words that have the same meaning as another word (e.g., instructor/teacher/educator, canine/dog, feline/cat, herbivore/vegetarian).

Antonyms refer to words that have the opposite meaning as another word (e.g., true/false, up/down, in/out, right/wrong).

Homonyms refer to words that are spelled the same (**homographs**) or sound the same (**homophones**) but mean different things (e.g., there/their/they're, two/too/to, principal/principle, plain/plane, (kitchen) sink/sink (down as in water)).

Syntax

With its origins from the Greek word, "syntaxis," which means arrangement, **syntax** is the study of phrase and sentence formation. The study of syntax focuses on the ways in which specific words can be combined to create coherent meaning. For example: the simple rearrangement of the words, "I can run," is different from the question, "Can I run?" which is also different from the meaningless, "Run I can."

The following methods can be used to teach syntax:

- Proper Syntax Modeling: Students do not need to be corrected for improper syntax. Instead, they should be shown ways to rephrase what they said with proper syntax. If a student says, "Run I can," then the teacher should say, "Oh, you can run how fast?" This puts syntax in place with conversational skills.

- Open-Ended Sentences: Students can complete open-ended sentences with proper syntax both orally and in written format, or they can correct sentences that have improper syntax so that they make sense.

- Listening for Syntax: Syntax is auditory. Students can often hear a syntax error before they can see it in writing. Teachers should have students use word cards or word magnets to arrange and rearrange simple sentences and read them aloud to check for syntax.

- Repetition: Syntax can be practiced by using songs, poems, and rhymes for repetitive automation.

Pragmatics

Pragmatics is the study of what words mean in certain situations. It helps to understand the intentions and interpretations of intentions through words used in human interaction. Different listeners and situations call for different language and intonations of language. When people engage in a conversation, it is usually to convey a certain message, and the message (even using the same words) can change depending on the setting and the audience. The more fluent the speaker, the more success she or he will have in conveying the intended message.

The following methods can be used to teach pragmatics:

- When students state something incorrectly, respond to what they intended to say. For instance, if a student says, "That's how it didn't happen." Then the teacher might say, "Of course, that's not how it happened." Instead of putting students on defense by being corrected, this method puts them at ease and helps them learn.

- Role-playing conversations with different people in different situations can help teach pragmatics. For example, pretend playing can be used where a situation remains the same but the audience changes, or the audience stays the same but the situations change. This can be followed with a discussion about how language and intonations change too.

- Different ways to convey a message can be used, such as asking vs. persuading, or giving direct vs. indirect requests and polite vs. impolite messages.

- Various non-verbal signals can be used to see how they change pragmatics. For example, students can be encouraged to use mismatched words and facial expressions, such as angry words while smiling or happy words while pretending to cry.

Independent Word-Learning Strategies

Students can have fun learning new words within the classroom. However, they will also need to learn words independently so that they will engage in more self-sustained reading. There are several independent word-learning strategies you can teach students to get the ball rolling.

Structural/Morphemic Analysis

When children are presented with an unfamiliar word, they use **morphemic analysis**, which looks at the root or origin of the word to interpret its meaning. As you may recall, morphemes are the most important units of words. Morphology consists of studying the combination of a prefix and suffix (creating an **affix**). Teaching students to create word matrices that divide morphemes into units and then having them define what each part means is a good tactic. They can do this on their own with new words as they learn them.

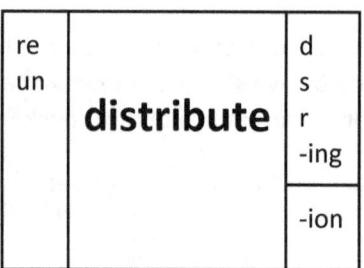

Contextual Analysis

Contextual analysis in reading involves figuring out what a word means by interpreting the text around it. This is commonly known as *picking up on context clues*. Students can do this by asking themselves what the paragraph or other parts of sentences were written about. Tell them to be mindful of the subject matter they are reading.

Print and Digital Resources

Teaching students to use print and digital resources is also a great way to help them learn new terms. They can make it a habit to either keep a physical copy or virtually bookmark a dictionary or thesaurus. That way, when they run into words they don't know while reading, they can simply look them up.

Context clues are also important here because many words have multiple meanings. Therefore, children will have to infer which definition is appropriate based on what they're reading.

Using all of these strategies will make your students stronger readers. They will become more confident and more likely to read on their own frequently.

Timing of Teaching New Vocabulary

When teaching your students new words, the most important factor is timing. Teaching words before students encounter them in a text helps students avoid confusion while reading. This method is useful for students who struggle with reading comprehension, and it can help make complex texts less overwhelming. For example, you might want to pre-teach words before your students read a book that includes many new scientific words. However, this teaching method can easily become boring. Make sure to engage students by giving examples, using the word in context, and using pictures for younger students.

Teaching students words as they encounter them in the text is useful because it is easier to learn words in context instead of relying on a definition. However, this method will be too disruptive if the text is full of new words. So, while a teacher could certainly teach words like "simultaneous" as they appear in a novel, teaching a long list of scientific words as they appear would break up the reading too much and frustrate the students.

Teaching words after students have completed the reading is useful when you are teaching children how to define new words by themselves. For example, the teacher could have students write down words they do not understand and look them up in a dictionary.

Strategies for Independent Vocabulary Acquisition

Teachers should also teach students word learning strategies so that they can gain vocabulary by themselves. Here are some effective strategies:

- Teaching students how to use dictionaries enables them to learn words independently. You can engage students by having them collect and define new words in a text, or by holding competitions to see who can use the dictionary faster.

- Contextual clues are the elements of a text that surround a word and hint at its meaning. For example, consider the following sentence: "He decided to litigate, so he hired a lawyer." A student could guess that "litigate" means "sue" by recognizing the cause-and-effect relationship between "decided to litigate" and "hired a lawyer." Another example of a contextual clue is contrast. If a student reads that "dogs are energetic, but cats are lethargic," they can use the word "but" to determine that "lethargic" is the opposite of "energetic."

- **Morphemic analysis** is defining words by breaking them into parts. A morpheme is a word part or unit of meaning; for example, the word "tirelessness" includes the morphemes "tire," "less," and "ness." If students know that "less" means "without" and "ness" turns adjectives into nouns, they can deduce the meaning of "tirelessness."

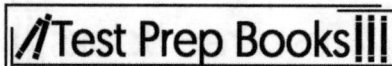

Strategies for Understanding and Pronouncing New Words

When using **contextual strategies**, students are introduced to new words indirectly within a sentence or paragraph. Contextual strategies require students to infer the meaning of a word by utilizing semantic and contextual clues.

Appositives and parenthetical elements can be very effective contextual strategies. **Appositives** are words that define or add meaning to a term that directly precedes them. An example of a sentence that includes apposition is: "Strawberries, heart-shaped and red berries, are delicious when eaten right off of the vine." In this sentence, the definition of strawberries ("heart shaped and red berries") directly follows the term and is introduced with and closes with a comma. **Parenthetical elements** are specific types of appositives that add details to a term but not necessarily a definition. For example: "My cat, the sweetest in the whole world, didn't come home last night." In this sentence, the parenthetical element ("the sweetest in the whole world") further describes the cat but does not provide a definition of the word "cat."

Structural analysis skills are beneficial in the pronunciation of new words. When readers use **structural analysis**, they recognize affixes or roots as meaningful parts within a word. When a new word does not contain parts that are recognized by a student, the reader can use phonic letter–sound patterns to divide the word into syllables. The word parts can then be combined to yield the proper pronunciation.

Word maps are visual organizers that promote structural analysis skills for vocabulary development. They may require students to provide definitions, synonyms, antonyms, and pictures for given vocabulary terms. Alternatively, **morphological maps** may be used to relate words that share a common morpheme. Similarly, **word webs** are used to compare and classify a list of words. Word webs show relationships between new words and a student's background knowledge. The main concept is in the center of the word web while secondary and tertiary terms stem off from it.

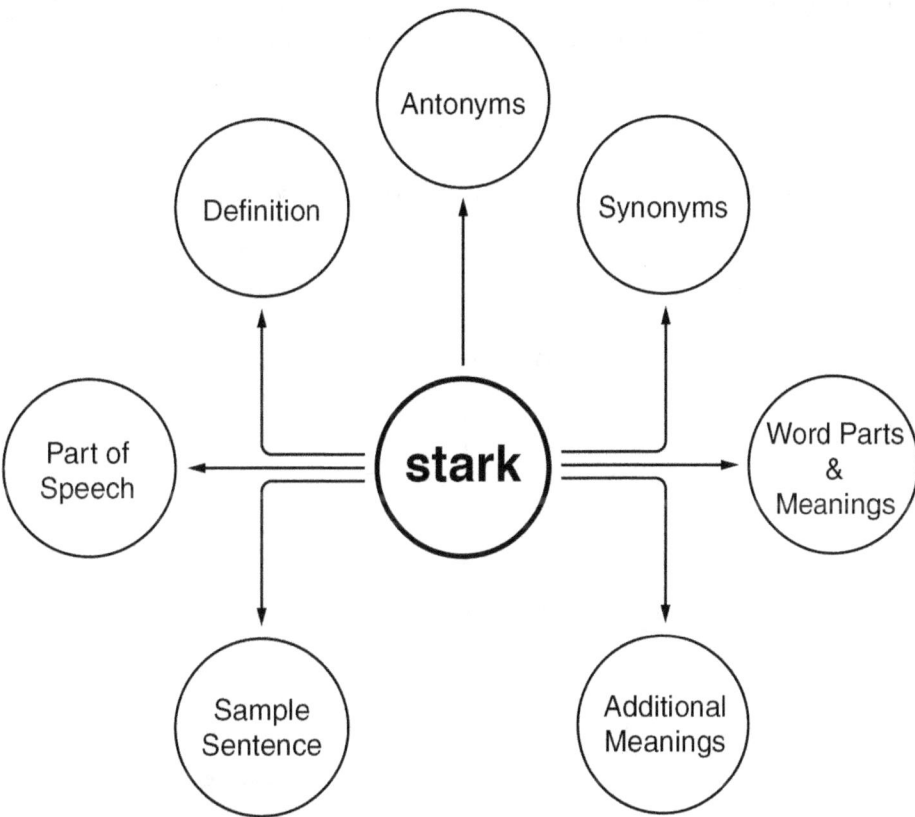

The table below identifies additional ways in which teachers can help students independently define unfamiliar words or words with multiple meanings:

Strategy	Examples
By Definition: Look up the word in a dictionary or thesaurus. Helps students realize that a single word can have multiple meanings.	Her favorite fruit to eat was a date. He went on a date with his girlfriend.
By Example: Invite students to offer their own examples or to state their understanding of your examples.	A myth is a story attempting to explain a natural phenomenon, such as the story of Prometheus to understand fire.
By Synonym: Understand that words have many different meanings. Some words are better synonyms than others.	She was very happy that day; her face was *radiant* with joy.
By Antonym: Teach student to look for words that have opposite meanings if the context of the sentence calls for its opposite.	Hannah was not happy that day; she was, in fact, very *depressed*.
By Apposition: Apposition is when the definition is given within the sentence.	The mango, a round, yellow, juicy fruit with an enormous seed in the middle, was ripe enough to eat.

Strategy	Examples
By Origin: Identify Greek and Latin roots to figure out meanings of words.	In the word *hypertension*, the root "*hyper*" is a Greek word meaning "above" or "over."
By Context: Identifying what a word means by the surrounding text.	Water evaporates when it becomes hot, and the liquid turns into gas.

Promoting Word Consciousness and Motivation to Learn New Words

Word consciousness can be developed through structural analysis of word parts and words origins. Identification of word segments will enable students to master new words more readily.

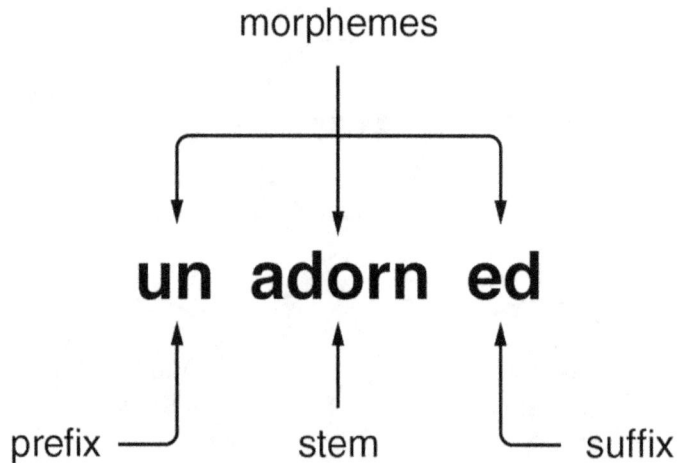

Students can develop a love of words through word games, which create a safe environment to take linguistic risks and feel successful. Examples include sight word games, word memory games, or games that require students to create new words using an assigned list of affixes and roots.

A **word sort** is an example of a word game that can be used to develop word consciousness. Using a set of word cards prepared by the teacher, students decide how to separate the cards into categories. Students are then asked to explain why they grouped a set of words together.

Students also learn to love words by sharing new and interesting words they encounter through independent reading or by learning new words taught explicitly by the teacher. Students can share new words on an online word blog or word cloud, a word wall within the classroom, or a word list contained within a notebook. These tools help to personalize vocabulary instruction while improving students' flexibility and fluency.

Schema development for easier word acquisition can be developed by dividing these word lists into categories based on similarities or differences. The list of new words should be referred to often in order to increase the students' exposure. To further strengthen comprehension, students should be required to utilize the words in writing and discussion activities.

Scaffolding

English Language Learners (ELLs) or students with varying dialects may need alternate methods of instruction when it comes to learning standard American English. **Scaffolding** refers to techniques that allow students to progress toward a greater level of understanding on an increasingly independent level. The teacher will help the student by gradually removing aid until the student can perform the task on their own. Although there are many different scaffolding techniques, a few common ones are presented below.

Connecting New Information to Prior Learning
When using the process of scaffolding, it is important to guide ELL students through the activities from the start. Teachers will determine what level of aid to give students depending on their language level. One important method of scaffolding is using previous experience to connect to new information. Teachers should be knowledgeable of students' cultures and world experiences in order to synthesize new and old information. Cultural relevance in the ELL framework is crucial for the student to understand the importance of what is being taught.

Pre-Teach Academic Vocabulary Outright
Another method of scaffolding is the practice of teaching vocabulary before full English language immersion takes place. Again, a collaborative effort will be most effective for this sort of learning experience. Have students work together to understand the vocabulary word, its meaning, and its idiomatic expressions; this enables them to learn vocabulary while also engaging in proximal social interactions. Word walls are suggested at all levels because they help students pronounce unfamiliar words and give them visual and auditory contact with the word.

Make Lessons Visual by Using Graphic Organizers
Visual aids are another helpful tool when scaffolding; they can help students develop creativity and work with others to assist collaboratively in each other's creativity and ideas. Graphic organizers include webs, Venn diagrams, story boards, KWL charts, spider maps, and charts, all of which help students organize information and develop higher-level thinking.

Engage English Learners in Discourse
Practicing language "out loud" creates a stimulating environment wherein the student can collaboratively work with others to immerse themselves in social and academic discourse. It is important to include academic language in verbal activities since it is harder to learn and requires a structured environment facilitated by the instructor. Engagement in academic conversations can come before or during social conversations. Social conversation may come easier, but academic conversation is important because it aids in research, writing, and career development.

Comprehension Development

Tools to Help Students Understanding Appropriately Complex Texts

Teach your students to annotate texts by highlighting and making notes in the margins. For example, you might have students read a confusing passage, then annotate it by highlighting the most important pieces of information and defining difficult words. By annotating texts, students learn to recognize central points and research words or background information that they do not understand.

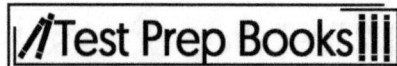

Teach your students to take notes. For students who are just learning to take notes, it may be helpful to practice reading a text as a class and making notes on the board. Teach your students useful skills like summarizing, picking out main points, and outlining arguments. For example, you could read a passage aloud and ask all the students to take notes. You could then have the class compare notes and write a collaborative summary of the text.

Have students apply metacognition to their comprehension by identifying the elements of a text that they cannot understand. For example, if a student says, "I don't understand this book," ask them to think about the specific aspects that confuse them and build a more detailed phrase like "I don't understand what happens in chapter four," or "I can't understand this word."

Assessing Reading Comprehension

Being able to assess children's reading comprehension levels is essential to creating well-informed instructional planning. How you interpret the results will determine which students require more or less assistance in the classroom.

As previously discussed, there are both formal and informal reading assessments. These tests have different formats, types of content, and allotted completion times, which can cause high variability in results from students. Therefore, the instructor must figure out the best strategies to interpret the results fairly.

Formal reading comprehension tests cannot measure the skills children used to complete them. For instance, a child could simply make educated guesses on multiple-choice questions; they could end up with a high score by chance even if they did not put much thought into that section.

A standardized test cannot tell you which section a student struggled the most with and had to spend more time on. The educator can observe these things throughout the school year through in-class assignments and regular testing that does not lump all of the examination methods together. They can also conduct individual testing sessions to observe each child's comprehension levels.

Reading comprehension tests are a fact of life for educators. To best understand the results, the tests should be reputable and reliable. Also, make sure students are exposed to a variety of tests. See which topics appear to be their favorites, and plan activities accordingly. Differentiated intervention strategies, such as setting reading goals, doing group projects, practicing sight words, reading aloud, and journaling, should be implemented. These types of activities help identify students' comprehension strengths and weaknesses.

Factors Affecting Reading Comprehension

The **National Early Literacy Panel (NELP)** studied the direct correlation between language skills, vocabulary development, grammar, and reading comprehension. The NELP found that children's vocabulary and grammar knowledge is reflected in their speech. Mastering both of these skills is also important to reading comprehension.

Oral language and listening skills are good indicators for how well-read children are. In fact, observing how well they speak can also indicate whether they are reading material that is sufficiently complex. Children who are good listeners tend to have better language and reading decoding skills than others.

As students progress through different grade levels, their academic language skills should continue to develop. This is where the different types of reading comprehension play a role. Students should be able to understand what specific academic terms mean in the appropriate context. They will be exposed to more complex topics as they advance, and they should be able to understand instructions better. Grammar and vocabulary are central to how students decode the new concepts they have learned in advanced grades.

When students apply personal experiences to their reading, they exhibit **background knowledge**. They can recall the characteristics of other texts and apply their prior literary experiences to the new curriculum. The capability to retain and convey previous knowledge is representative of **reading fluency**; fluent readers are able to retain what they have read and quickly analyze texts. Fluency is usually an effect of reading often.

Eventually, students should be able to **self-monitor** their reading comprehension levels, recognizing when they are struggling with particular words or an overall text, and they should seek out ways to improve. Their level of English language proficiency is directly related to self-monitoring. Readers at both poor and advanced proficiency levels will be aware of how well they can read. Some students may become frustrated by their lack of skills and stop self-sustained reading altogether. They could also become less attentive in class.

Literary and Informational Texts

Teaching Literary Texts

The strategies for teaching literary texts often overlap with those for teaching informational texts, but there are a few key differences.

While guiding questions are just as helpful for literature as for informational texts, the questions for literary texts can be more open-ended and offer opportunities for students to express opinions on the reading. For example, teachers can ask questions like, "Do you think the character made the right decision?" or "How does the novel's setting contribute to the plot?" Teach students to engage with the material and back up their claims.

Teach students to support their analysis of literature with textual evidence. **Textual evidence** is material from the literary text itself. A student who bases an argument on historical facts, the author's life, or personal experience is not using textual evidence; however, someone who argues from the events and wording of a novel is using textual evidence. Teaching students about textual evidence helps them read closely and learn to form unbiased arguments.

Teach students to map stories and identify literary elements. **Freytag's pyramid** is the most common method of mapping the critical developments in a story. It is particularly useful for helping students understand the important events in a novel. For example, you could have students map *To Kill a*

Mockingbird individually, and then discuss the maps as a class. Students should also know terms like "setting" and "theme" so that they can talk and write about their ideas.

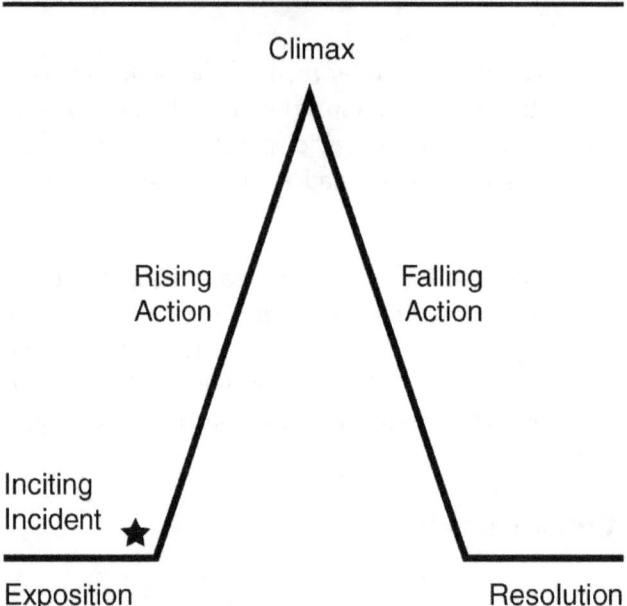

While there are correct and incorrect answers to questions about the factual events in a literary text, the answers to questions about themes and the text's message are not so simple. Instead of offering definitive readings on what the text means, facilitate discussion and make suggestions. Studying literature is a great way for students to develop creativity and argumentative skills, and you do not want to squelch that process by being too authoritative.

Teaching Students to Read Informational Texts

Here are some strategies for teaching students to understand and analyze informational texts.

Before the class reads a text, give students a few guiding questions and ask them to find the answers in the reading. For example, suppose that your students are about to read a book about the salmon lifecycle. You might ask them, "How many times do salmon travel during their lives?" and "Where do salmon die?" Approaching the text with guiding questions helps structure students' thoughts and teaches them to take notes. This method is particularly useful for young students, as it takes the attention off the unimportant details that sometimes fascinate young readers and redirects it to the central points of the text.

Teach students to summarize information. For example, you could ask students to take notes on the most important points in a text and then write a summary. Younger students do better with simple oral summaries, while older students can handle more complicated written work. Summarizing is a great way to improve comprehension. It also tests analysis skills, as students need to discern which points are important and which are just details.

Ask students to develop questions about the text. For instance, you could ask each student to read the assigned text and then bring one question about it to class. Teaching students to generate questions helps them be curious about reading and promotes creative thinking. This is particularly helpful when teaching older students to analyze more complex texts, as it teaches them to form arguments and evaluate material.

Teach students to form connections between the text and other material. For instance, students could read one book about Russia and another about Spain and then compare the two countries.

Alternatively, teachers can ask students to draw comparisons between the information in a text and their life experiences. This method is particularly effective for younger students, as it boosts engagement. For example, after reading a book about beavers, a teacher might ask their students whether any of them has seen a beaver. The class could then compare the information in the book to the students' experiences.

Evaluating and Sequencing Texts for Reading Instruction

Choosing Reading Materials and Curricula

When choosing curricula to use in your classroom, there are a number of factors to consider.

Consider the needs of your students and choose materials that will accommodate those needs. For example, if you are teaching a group of students who are repeating a year because they struggled to learn reading, find materials that offer plenty of resources for struggling learners and children with learning disabilities. Alternatively, if you are teaching gifted students, you need a curriculum that is fast-paced and activities that will allow students to explore their individual interests.

Find materials that offer flexibility for the teacher and students. For example, a good curriculum will offer ideas on alternative teaching materials, assessment strategies, and activities so that teachers can tailor the materials to the needs of their class. Having a flexible curriculum also allows you to modify the level of your materials for students who are above and below the average level in your class.

Make sure that the materials you choose are clear and appealing to students. Avoid choosing curriculum with unclear explanations. You should also make sure that your materials do not include elements that will confuse students or distract them from learning the material, such as outdated language or disorienting formatting. Finally, the reading materials should be interesting so that students are motivated to read and learn from their studies.

Ensure that your materials integrate well with any assessments you have planned. For example, if your school requires a certain test at winter break, make sure that you will cover the materials your students will be tested on before the exam.

Determining the Effectiveness of Reading Materials

Make sure that the materials you choose are consistent with current research on reading. Keeping up with current research will prevent you from using outdated curricula, and it will make you aware of new and improved teaching methods. However, the newest methods are not always the best. Instead of trying to incorporate every trending idea, look for materials that use methods that are backed by a wide body of research.

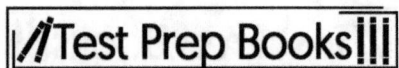

Consider whether the materials offer a balanced approach to reading instruction. You should choose materials that teach all reading skills well instead of focusing unduly on some while ignoring others. For example, a bad curriculum might focus on vocabulary and reading speed so much that it neglects to teach students phonics. A good curriculum, however, teaches basic skills like phonics while also incorporating vocabulary, comprehension exercises, and writing skills.

Look at the lesson sequence and consider whether the material is organized in a way that is conducive to learning. For example, a bad program might start teaching complex phonograms (like "sh" as in "ship") before it has finished teaching basic consonants (like "s" and "h"). This design would make it difficult for students to learn, because they would have to recognize letters in phonograms before they recognized them in isolation. A good program will organize the material so that students grasp fundamental concepts before encountering more complex ones.

Three Levels of Reading Comprehension

Literal Comprehension
Literal comprehension refers to the reader's ability to understand the actual meaning of texts. This is not meant to be complicated. It means literally understanding the facts, setting, plot, etc. of what is being read.

To bolster literal comprehension, show students how to ask pertinent questions. When they are reading stories, children should learn to ask who the characters are, what happened, where the story is taking place, and in what order the events occurred.

Inferential Comprehension
Inferential comprehension requires students to understand the hidden context or unstated meaning of a text. They should be able to explain why an action occurred and what they think will happen next.

When it comes to inferential comprehension, children need to recall the facts that occurred in the story and what those facts represent. They should ask the following questions:

- Why did this happen?
- How might the characters feel?
- What might happen next?
- How important is "X" character?

Evaluative Comprehension
Evaluative comprehension can be a matter of opinion; the student will make a judgment about the moral or definitive meaning of a piece of writing.

Evaluative comprehension involves questions about the moral of the story. Students primarily need to ask, "what does this story teach us?" If there is a conflict in the story, they need to ask, "how can this be solved? Is "X" character right or wrong?" The students should also freely express how they felt about the story and if they like the way it was written.

These three levels of comprehension are all part of critical thinking. Critical thinking allows students to identify if there are any biases in a story. They will be able to organize the information they have learned to form stronger opinions about what they read. They will also become stronger readers.

Critical thinking is difficult to teach because it depends on the comprehension skills of the people doing the thinking. Different types of reading material also call for different types of analysis. As teachers, your best bet is to encourage critical thinking at every opportunity. Standard strategies that encourage critical thinking include assigning various types of reading materials and topics, asking students to recall what they have read, and giving assignments that make them elaborate on the reading.

Engaging Students in Discussion

Two great ways to engage students in discussion are literature circles and discussion circles. Literature circles are groups of students who read the same text independently and meet to discuss their findings. Depending on the needs of your class, you may choose to assign books to your groups or allow them to choose their own.

Discussion circles are similar to literature circles, but they focus on discussing a topic rather than the text itself. Depending on your students' ages and abilities, you can guide the discussion to be about anything from basic facts (e.g., summarizing what happened in a text) to abstract ideas (e.g., discussing the themes of a novel). For example, after reading *Huckleberry Finn*, students may discuss the immorality of slavery.

Debates are also a good way for students to practice building convincing arguments. Teachers can break the class into groups and have them prepare arguments supporting contradictory claims. For example, students could divide into a group arguing that *Jane Eyre* is a feminist novel, and another arguing that it is not. Depending on your topic and how popular each viewpoint is, you can allow students to choose their side or assign them randomly. Having students argue for the side they do not believe builds objectivity and critical thinking, so it is not an inferior option.

Metacognition and Critical Thinking Skills

Metacognition is thinking about your own thoughts or learning process. For example, a student who thinks, "When I think ___, I am making an assumption," is practicing metacognition. Metacognition is important because it enables people to evaluate their ideas objectively and determine whether they are valid. Metacognition can also help students think about the way they learn and improve their learning strategies. For example, a student who realizes that they can memorize things faster by writing them down can implement that technique to study efficiently.

Critical thinking is a broad term that refers to students' ability to evaluate materials and form logical conclusions. For example, a student who reads a Shakespeare play and analyzes it is thinking critically; however, a student who identifies Shakespeare as the author is just stating a fact, not thinking critically.

Here are some techniques that you can use to help your students develop metacognition and critical thinking skills:

- When students pose an opinion, ask them why they have that opinion. For example, ask, "You've said that you really disliked the novel. Why do you think you feel that way?" This technique provides a way for students to think through their own thought process. However, teachers should be wary of asking too many questions; if students have to defend every single opinion, they will become frustrated.

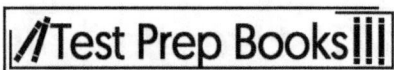

- Model metacognition by talking through your own thought processes. For example, you might write textual evidence on the board and then map your thoughts as you analyze it.

- Ask students about how they experience learning and encourage them to use their observations to study more efficiently. For example, you could ask your students to think about whether they are more visual or auditory learners, and then ask them to brainstorm ways that they could use their strengths to learn new vocabulary words.

- Teach your students to identify logical fallacies. A **fallacy** is a way of using logic poorly, which may result in a false conclusion. For example, the claim, "Dickens criticizes the government, so he must be an anarchist," contains a fallacy because it presents a false dilemma: wholeheartedly supporting the government and being an anarchist are not the only possible viewpoints.

Comprehension Strategies for Complex Literary and Informational Texts

Reading material will grow more technical and complex between kindergarten and grade 6. Some students will adapt well to the new material, and others will struggle a bit with the nuances. The following are some research-based rereading practices to engage students who are having trouble understanding complicated texts.

Instructors can ask their students **text-dependent questions**, which require students to go back and reread the text in order to find answers. After diving deeper into the text, students should be able to craft thoughtful answers to the instructors' questions. Some examples of text-dependent questions are those that ask the meanings of words, the writer's point of view, and the purpose of the text.

Annotation, or the practice of highlighting or marking parts of the writing that seem important, also requires careful reading. Teachers can help students do this by telling them what concepts to look for in the writing. You could provide a helpful annotation worksheet, which lists what readers should look out for. Students could also write questions about parts of the text that need clarifying.

Annotation can also be used to deconstruct grammatically complex sentences. To do this, students can be asked to identify the sentence that gives them trouble and identify the nouns, verbs, adjectives, and so forth, by circling them. Then, ask them to identify the subject and verb. See if they can infer from the surrounding text what difficult words mean. If they can't, they can look them up.

Educators can also reread the text with the students and ask them what they think it means. More than likely, they will interpret it differently. Having them write down their perspectives and then read them aloud is an exercise that could spark in-class conversation. Teachers should use this opportunity to encourage collaboration between students. Breaking students into groups and giving them text-dependent questions is another exercise that will help spark discussion.

All of these strategies are effective at deciphering complex writing. Use them to encourage intentional reading and group communication.

Independent and Reflective Reading

Students who engage in independent reading are able to read, retain, and analyze the text that they have read completely independent of outside aid. It also allows them to feel as if they had a choice in picking their own text to read, instead of the feeling that it has been chosen for them. Reflective reading is the ability to absorb text with a sense of analysis in mind. Here are some examples of questions students can ask themselves while engaged in reflective reading:

- What am I reading?
- Why am I reading this?
- What is the author trying to tell me?
- Why is this character acting in a certain way?

Encouraging independent and reflective reading is dependent on the type of literature instructors choose to introduce in their classrooms. Culture, race, age, and reading level are all very important characteristics to keep in mind when choosing texts to have in the classroom for independent readers. If some students are ELLs, acquire some texts that are bilingual or ELL-appropriate. Choose authors with various ethnic backgrounds rather than the most popular books at the time. Find authors who have similar cultures to the students in the classroom. Choose difficult books for your advanced students and appropriate books for the students who still struggle with reading. Students will have greater motivation to read and understand the language if they can relate to the message of the text.

Strategies for Effective Reading

Skimming for Gist
Sometimes assigned reading is incredibly lengthy and complicated, making it harder for some readers to get through the passages. To deduce quickly what the information is telling them, they should learn to skim for gist. The **gist** is the overall concept of the passage. By skimming, readers can move through the text and make note of key sections along the way. To **skim**, students should read the first paragraph of the text, look for key words related to that paragraph in the body, and then read the final paragraph.

Scanning for Specific Information
Scanning text involves looking for more specific important information such as names, dates, and times. If students have some background knowledge about the topic, it is helpful to note what questions they might ask or specific facts they would expect to see beforehand. This will make the scanning go quickly.

Focused Reading
In **focused reading**, which is usually conducted in a quiet environment with few distractions, students should proceed slowly through each section of the content, reading each and every word. The entire document does not have to be read at once—the reader can break it up into sections, specifically focusing on one or more sections per day at a set time. Setting small reading goals and taking breaks is essential to focused reading.

Rereading for Understanding
To glean important information from a passage, students should **reread** certain sentences and ask questions about what they mean. A student can reread these sentences as many times as they need to. The instructor can have them stop and look up unfamiliar terms and discuss what is happening with their classmates. They can also look up the terms independently. In addition, the teacher can ask the students to reread a sentence multiple times and placed their books down and tell the class what they have just read. This will help with memorization. You can also give them writing assignments focused on what they have reread.

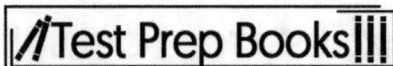

Genres of Literary and Informational Texts

Reading is fundamental to learning. Reading nurtures imagination, critical thinking, communication skills, and social competence. Many children are drawn to the allure of reading and often their attention is captivated by a certain type of book or books about a particular personal interest. It is important to introduce them to an eclectic selection of texts. Cultural knowledge, a more intricate worldview, and a host of new vocabulary can be built through the experience of diverse literature. Reading a wide range of writing styles brings students into contact with many characters and lifestyles. Reading varied texts sparks different emotions and teaches a variety of means of expression. In this way, children deepen social and emotional skills. In short, reading a wide variety of texts produces a well-rounded education and prepares children for their experience of the world.

Fiction
Fiction is imaginative text that is invented by the author. Fiction is characterized by the following literary elements:

- **Characters:** the people, animals, aliens, or other living figures the story is about
- **Setting:** the location, surroundings, and time the story takes place in
- **Conflict:** a dilemma the characters face either internally or externally
- **Plot:** the sequence of the story, or its rise and fall of action
- **Resolution:** the solution to the conflict
- **Point of view:** the lens through which the reader experiences the story
- **Theme:** the moral to the story or the message the author sends to the reader

Historical Fiction
Historical fiction is a story that occurs in the past and uses a realistic setting and authentic time period characters. Historical fiction usually has some historically accurate events mixed and balanced with invented plot and characters.

Science Fiction
Science fiction is an invented story that occurs in the future or an alternate universe. It often deals with space, time travel, robots or aliens, and highly advanced technology.

Fantasy
Fantasy is a subgenre of fiction that involves magic or supernatural elements and/or takes place in an imaginary world. Examples include talking animals, superheroes rescuing the day, or characters taking on a mythical journey or quest.

Mystery and Adventure
Mystery fiction is a story that involves a puzzle or crime to be solved by the main characters. The mystery is driven by suspense and foreshadowing. The reader must sift through clues and distractions to solve the puzzle with the protagonist. **Adventure stories** are driven by the risky or exciting action that happens in the plot.

Realistic and Contemporary Fiction
Realistic fiction depends on the author portraying the world without speculation. The characters are ordinary, and the action could happen in real life. The conflict often involves growing up, family life, or learning to cope with some significant emotion or challenge.

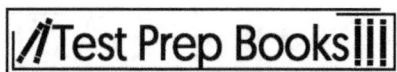

Nonfiction Literature
Nonfiction literature is true and accurate in detail. It can cover virtually any topic in the natural world. Nonfiction writers conduct research and carefully organize facts before writing. Nonfiction has the following subgenres:

- **Informational Text**: This is text written to impart information to the reader. It may have literary elements such as charts, graphs, indexes, glossaries, or bibliographies.

- **Persuasive Text**: This is text that is meant to sway the reader to have a particular opinion or take a particular action.

- **Biographies and autobiographies**: These texts that tells intimate details of someone's life. If an author writes the text about someone else, it is a biography. If the author writes it about himself or herself, it is an autobiography.

- **Communicative text**: This is text used to communicate with another person. It includes such texts as emails, formal and informal letters, and social media posts. This content often consists of two-sided dialogue between people.

Drama
Drama is any writing that is intended to be performed in front of an audience, such as scripts for plays, TV, and movies. Dialogue and action are central to convey the author's theme. **Comedy** is any drama designed to be funny or lighthearted. **Tragedy** is any drama designed to be serious or sad.

Poetry
Poetry is text that is written in verse and has a rhythmic cadence. It often involves descriptive imagery, rhyming stanzas, and beautiful mastery of language. It is often personal, emotional, and introspective.

Folklore
Folklore is literature that has been handed down from generation to generation by word of mouth. Folklore is not based in fact but in unsubstantiated beliefs. It is often very important to a culture or custom.

Differentiating Instruction in Text Comprehension

In any classroom, there will be students who fall behind or are at risk for struggling in the future. Here are some ways to recognize these students, preventing failure before it happens and helping students who are behind get back on track.

Implement screening assessments at the start of the school year. For example, you might administer the Informal Reading Inventory during the first few weeks of class to determine whether any of your students are at risk and would benefit from intervention.

Build communication with your students' parents and suggest ways for parents of at-risk students to improve their children's performance, such as reading with them or supervising their homework. Often, parents who know that their child is struggling at school can take steps to help the student work through these issues at home before they become a bigger problem. For example, telling a couple that their son is performing poorly on spelling tests might enable the parents to motivate him to practice at home and catch up with the rest of the class.

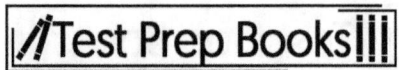

Make sure that at-risk students are receiving adequate peer support. Peer support is the help that students receive from other students. For example, if a struggling student asks another student to explain something, they are asking for peer support. Peer support is important because it increases the engagement in your classroom and builds a sense of community and responsibility. You can encourage students to help each other by seating at-risk students near high performers, implementing a buddy system, and breaking students into groups.

Scaffolding is a method of making students' workload seem less overwhelming by dividing it into manageable sections. Instead of assigning all the work at once and letting students either accomplish it or fail, teachers break the learning into steps and help students accomplish each one. For example, a teacher might scaffold by teaching the unfamiliar vocabulary in a text before the students read it. Scaffolding is a great way of preventing confusion and helping students with poor organization skills stay on track.

Multisensory instruction is a method of integrating touch, sight, and hearing to teach new skills. For example, a teacher might have a student draw new vocabulary words after reading or hearing them. By appealing to multiple areas of the brain, multisensory instruction builds strong memory cues and puts students with different strengths on an equal playing field.

Comprehension of Literary Texts

Assessing Comprehension and Analysis of Complex Literary Texts

<u>Comprehension</u>
Reading Aloud
Having students read specific passages out loud is a good way to see if they recognize common words and phrases. It will also highlight which words they are pronouncing correctly or incorrectly.

Retelling
Assign students different reading assignments that vary in complexity. After each assignment, ask them to recount what the texts were about and what stood out to them; ask text-specific questions to guide them. They can either write this information down or share it out loud in class. This will show if they were able to understand the stories and other assigned materials.

Formal Assessment
In Texas, students in grades 3–12 take what is known as the State of Texas Assessments of Academic Readiness (STAAR). As teachers of grades 3–6, you will have to prepare your students for STAAR. These tests analyze children's writing and reading skills. For the reading portion, they are provided different passages and then asked multiple-choice questions about what they read. Commonly asked questions address plot lines, settings, primary characters, and passage themes. Vocabulary knowledge is also assessed by asking them to identify the inferred meanings of certain words.

<u>Analysis</u>
The same techniques mentioned above can be used to see how well students understand various literature. Here are some more.

Spelling and Vocabulary

Address your students' analysis skills by giving them regular spelling and vocabulary tests that relate to their required reading. They should be able to decode words either by using context clues or by knowing how to look them up. Children often spell words the way they pronounce them; pop-up quizzes can show teachers what terms students know how to spell and pronounce correctly.

Writing

As students progress, introduce them to increasingly complex reading material. Ask them to write book reports, essays, and journal entries. Freewriting assignments in the classroom remove distractions and the ability to "Google" answers to questions. Children's critical thinking skills will be activated with these types of assignments. Teachers will be able to see who understood the texts and who did not.

Once you have assessed your students' comprehension and analysis skills, use the results to further inform your curriculum.

Interpret the Results of Assessments in Reading Comprehension and Analysis of Literary Texts

Keep in mind that no two students will read at exactly the same level. Assistance provided to students who are struggling will need to be differentiated according to their particular abilities.

Start by keeping a tally of each student's mistakes when reading or completing assignments. Ask yourself the following questions about your students:

- How many words did they mispronounce?
- Which specific words did they struggle with?
- What was the complexity of the reading assigned?
- Which terms were misspelled in their assignments and tests?

Organize this data however you see fit; some experts recommend using charts that record each student's progress over time as well as their class participation style. Over time, instructors will notice which students speak up in class and which tend to stay quiet.

Keep in mind all of the different learning styles (kinesthetic, auditory, etc.). Try different teaching methods to see who responds to what technique. For example, have all students work in small groups one day, and the next, organize some interpersonal instruction time with each. Then, allow them time to work individually. It should become clear who works best in each situation.

Using these strategies should enable teachers to come up with appropriate lesson plans. It is important that instruction is differentiated according to each student's needs so that they can improve their reading comprehension and analysis skills. It will also help teachers figure out which teaching techniques and assignments work best and which need to be improved.

Types of Children's Literature

The types of literature children are exposed to when they first start reading can vary by culture, social economics, and environmental factors. It is important that they are introduced to children's literature early on, no matter the genre. Most children's reading material has some of the following common features:

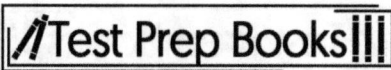

- Simple wording
- Images featuring children
- Child characters
- Repeated phrases
- Optimistic ending

There are different types of children's literature, and they all have defining characteristics. Below are the most common types of children's literature.

Folktales, Fables, and Fairy Tales
Folktales originated as orally shared stories between people of a common culture and include mythology or legend to describe past events. Fairy tales are types of folklore that are usually fantastical in nature, containing supernatural elements, such as mythological creatures or magic. Fables are shorter stories that include elements like talking animals or anthropomorphized objects that might highlight societal values. Folktales, fables, and fairy tales usually teach a lesson or moral.

Legends, Myths, and Tall Tales
Legends are usually based on historical information with mythical elements, while myths and tall tales are wildly exaggerated and often fictional. These stories tend to be centered on the actions of humans. They are usually told to explain natural occurrences, like the formation of lakes or mountains. They also tend to reaffirm values or common beliefs.

Nursery Rhymes
Nursery rhymes are songs or poems that are used to teach children new words or other bits of information. They often involve musical rhyming and repetition. The repetition, in particular, is used to help children remember these rhymes.

Poetry
Poems use descriptive words that help children visualize what they hear. They can rhyme, but they don't have to. Children's poems tend to be happy and uplifting. Like nursery rhymes, poetry can also involve repetition.

Drama
Children's dramas feature characters and dialogue. The plots are descriptive but simple enough for children to understand. The characters often have realistic personalities and emotions, which young readers identify in themselves.

Children's literature offers an array of story-telling options. Every culture has its own version of the genres mentioned above. When implementing them in the classroom, there is sure to be a type of story that appeals to every student.

Continuum of Development in Comprehension and Analysis of Literary Texts

Children's comprehension and analysis of literary texts will continue developing as they advance in age. The Texas Prekindergarten Guidelines and the Texas Essential Knowledge and Skills (TEKS) for English Language Arts and Reading (ELAR) highlight the skills that students need to improve their comprehension and analysis abilities.

Notably, the Prekindergarten Guidelines and TEKS for ELAR state that students should continually be able to identify literary plots and themes, make personal connections with those themes, identify sensory details, and recount the literature they have read. To meet these criteria, students will need to be able to do the following things.

Inferring and Making Predictions

When reading texts, children should be able to draw conclusions about the primary characters and series of events they have read about. They should be able to identify actions taken within the texts and how they affect the primary characters or overall plot. Picking up on clues while they are reading is crucial to inference. For example, when reading stories that feature a hero and a nemesis, children should be able to tell who is who from warning signs or context clues.

Providing Evidence

This step sometimes precedes inference and prediction. Students need to provide evidence for their predictions. They can do this by pointing out the facts. They should answer the following questions:

- What actions took place in the text?
- Who or what completed these actions?
- What were the results?

According to the Prekindergarten Guidelines and TEKS for ELAR, if children are reading content that provides instructions, they should be able to follow them. This can include recipes, stories that allow you to choose the ending, or texts that ask you to complete an activity.

Children should be able to analyze different types of texts with these skills. Their ability to make predictions and inferences demonstrates how well they comprehend what they read.

Reading Aloud

Reading aloud is one of the best things teachers can do with students. It helps improve their language skills, their ability to identify story elements, and their overall desire to read. Reading culturally relevant, high-quality texts aloud enables children to see themselves represented in the story. Students are also more likely to memorize key elements of the stories when they can make personal connections to them.

The texts should be appropriately complex so that students can understand basic story structures. Kindergarten and first graders are more amenable to picture books, while students in higher grades should be introduced to short stories, novellas, and articles that may not feature images.

There are a number of best practices teachers can use to engage students when reading aloud. These strategies help them understand the literary texts and their important parts.

Using puppets or other props to act out stories is a great way to keep children interested in the storylines. Not only can teachers use them while they read, but they can hand the props over to students after and ask them to reenact different scenes.

In addition to reenactments, children love making sound effects to stories. When reading a story like "The Three Little Pigs," for instance, teachers can ask students to "huff and puff" each time the wolf approaches a pig's house. Telling students to clap their hands or play musical instruments, like symbols or recorders, can be implemented similarly.

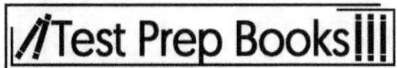

Children should be encouraged to ask questions during reading sessions. Teachers can set aside time after certain passages for asking questions. Instructors can also pose questions to the students during this time to see who was paying attention.

Many teachers create story maps and cards to use during read alouds. Story maps highlight the main parts of a story. Provide students with a print copy of a blank story map with specific questions about the parts of a story. During or after reading a story together, ask students to write in answers to these questions. Alternatively, you can draw a story map on a whiteboard and fill in the bubbles as you ask students the same questions.

Story cards feature pictures or phrases with characters or story plot points. To use them when reading aloud, ask the students to hold up the cards when certain characters appear or a certain action takes place. These cards can also be used to answer questions about what has occurred in the story or what the students think will happen next. Students can use these cards to reconstruct the stories later by putting them in sequential order.

To extend learning beyond read alouds, put children into literacy centers. Literacy centers are essentially workstations set up around the classroom focused on independent or group learning. These centers should each have a different activity. One might focus on group reading while another provides students with props to retell stories. At a writing workstation, students can create their own stories about the characters they just learned about.

Comprehension and Analysis of Complex Literary Texts

Students should be able to comprehend and analyze a broad range of literary texts. Understanding story elements, recognizing figurative language, and crafting appropriate responses to reading materials are just a few of the things students should learn to do as they increase their reading. One of a reading teacher's goals should be to help students analyze texts. There are a number of research-based strategies to help them do so.

The first thing instructors should do is observe their students' reading skills. Take note of which students are effective readers and which need a little more help. Regular in-class reading assignments and read alouds should help ascertain this information.

To help students begin comprehending texts, teachers should introduce them to the concept of metacognitive strategizing, which is the process of understanding one's own thought processes. To implement this strategy, teachers need to encourage students to ask questions of the texts that employ critical thinking. To start students off, give them a list of questions about the conflicts, settings, and morals presented in the stories. Then, ask them to identify areas of the texts they struggled to comprehend.

Rereading passages is a comprehension and analysis strategy. By going over parts of a story more than once, students have to confront the writing that they either did not understand or that stood out to them the most. After they have read the passages a certain number of times, ask students to rewrite them in their own words.

Teaching students to summarize is another comprehension and analysis technique. They can complete rewriting exercises here as well. Students just need to do three things when they employ this technique. They should recall what they read, identify the main point of the texts, and exclude unnecessary information. Summarizing does not have to take place after students have finished reading texts; they can do it as they go along. Eventually, this type of summarizing will be second nature, and students will be able to assess the texts without stopping.

Differentiating Instruction in the Comprehension and Analysis of Complex Literary Texts

When it comes to teaching methods, start with the basics. Breaking up reading material into chunks is incredibly helpful. Focus on one passage or one chapter at a time. Go over unknown vocabulary and quiz students on it. Take breaks in between reading sessions to discuss what has happened so far.

Students are never too old for visuals. In fact, taking a multimedia approach to teaching has been found to be effective for all grade levels. Use presentation technology like PowerPoint to outline the main concepts of the reading material. Incorporate videos. If the book being read in class was made into a miniseries or movie, see if you can acquire it and show it to the class. Use infographics and diagrams to break down the various parts of texts.

Teachers need to see how well students work individually and in groups. Assign them individual tasks, like creating a glossary of terms used in the reading. Then put them in different groups to come up with a story using those words. Do not assign students to the same groups all the time; mix them up so that they are exposed to learners of different backgrounds and personalities.

Depending on the grade, ask students to do some research about the authors they have read in class. Teach them how to find reliable resources on the computer or in the library.

Make learning fun for your students. Teachers can best address the comprehension abilities of each child when there is a large variety of learning activities.

Comprehension of Informational Texts

Differentiating Assessments in Reading Comprehension and Analysis

Just as texts have to be differentiated for students, so do assessments of those students' comprehension and analysis skills. Asking a standard set of questions for all texts, no matter the subject or complexity, is not the way to go because a student could effectively read one type of material but struggle with another. Here are some differentiation strategies teachers can use.

Provide students with a reading log worksheet or booklet. In this log, they should record information about what they read in class and at home, such as the author, the subject matter, and the student's thoughts on the text. The latter can be just a few short sentences or a list of words that students think when they read the text. At the end of each week, collect the logs and make note of what the children wrote. This will provide a look into whether they understood what they were reading or have other interpretations.

Young readers often respond well to journaling. Just like keeping a reading log, students are responsible for updating their journals with thoughts about the texts, but in more depth. Task them with writing at least one page about what they learned from the material they read. Teachers can also give students a writing prompt centered on the primary theme of the content.

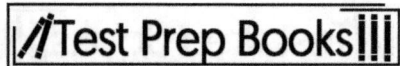

At some point, children learn to compare and contrast. Take advantage of this skill by having them compare and contrast the main elements or structures of two different stories. After reading each story, students should be asked to identify the beginning, middle, and end of each story in addition to the plot, setting, and conflict. Put these criteria into lists. After they are completed, compare the two lists. Ask specific questions about the key differences, such as, "How is character *A* different from character *B*? How did the first story begin differently from the second? Are these settings similar? If so, in what ways?"

These comprehension and analysis assessment methods depart from the usual multiple-choice question tests. Because they go more in depth, these tactics provide teachers with a better understanding of their students' reading levels.

Interpreting the Results of Assessments in Reading Comprehension and Analysis of Informational Texts

While teachers assess students' comprehension levels, they should take ample notes and record the assessment results. Then they will need to interpret the data, which will inform their instructional planning.

The most helpful, basic tactic teachers can use to interpret their assessment results is to organize it according to what they are looking for. Arrange this information in categories. The most common categories include text length, topic, complexity, and type.

Some instructors create Excel spreadsheets or Word tables and fill in this information under headings. There should be one spreadsheet per student. Pie charts, graphs, and other diagrams are good ways to display findings. The information recorded should reflect each student's performance in each category. For example, under the heading *length of texts*, note whether students exhibited better reading skills with short or long texts. Under *topics*, fill in which topics the students responded to the most.

Teachers should also track other common skills, such as vocabulary, spelling, writing ability, and pronunciation for each text. There is no need to create a whole new spreadsheet for this data--it can be added in on the same page. However, this must be consistent for each student's spreadsheet or tab. Under labels for each skill, note the students' performance. This can be the number of words spelled or pronounced incorrectly, their writing ability (poor, medium, advanced), and more.

If you need help making these spreadsheets or want to download a premade example, visit https://www.twinkl.com/resource/editable-tracking-assessment-spreadsheet-t2-t-10000532.

Teachers Pay Teachers is another reliable source for downloadable assessment spreadsheets: https://www.teacherspayteachers.com/Browse/Search:assessment%20data%20spreadsheet.

These spreadsheets are meant to help, not confuse. If organized correctly, teachers will see which areas students need some assistance with and which they excel at. Recording this data enables teachers to create targeted, differentiated activities that address students' strengths and weaknesses.

Different Types of Texts

Informational
Informational texts consist of nonfiction writing used to educate the audience about specific topics. Textbooks, news articles, and biographies are examples.

Persuasive
Persuasive writing is nonfiction used to convince readers to believe certain information or to purchase products. Advertisements and other marketing materials, newspapers, reviews, and reports are all persuasive.

Digital
Hyperlinks, videos, interactive maps, slideshow action buttons, GIFs, and graphics are all features of digital texts. They capture the reader's attention and usually lead them to more information about the text.

Multimodal
As the name implies, multimodal texts employ a combination of modes to present information. Oral storytelling, slideshows, videos, websites, performance art, and graphic novels all fall into this category.

Students will be introduced to most, if not all, of these texts in and out of the classroom. Over time, they will develop preferences for some more than others. Using a variety of content to teach makes the classroom an interesting place to be.

TEKS for ELAR Guidelines for Comprehension and Analysis of Informational Texts

The TEKS for ELAR have a few requirements for developing students' comprehension and analysis of informational texts. In particular, teachers should prepare students to:

- Recognize traits and structure such as the main idea, context, and sequential order
- Be able to effectively read and write informational texts
- Annotate informational texts

Teachers are expected to introduce students to various modes and genres of texts. Students should be prepared to speak, write, and critically think about their reading material. The TEKS for ELAR expect students to be able to respond adequately to questions about this content.

These requirements are for elementary students. They are non-grade specific. However, teachers should appropriately tailor their instruction using suitable mediums. Depending on their ages, children will be amenable to different types of texts. For example, kindergarten through second graders may prefer patterned books and videos, while children in grades three and up may respond best to chapter books.

The TEKS for ELAR places emphasis on students' capacities to read, write, and expound on literature and informational texts. Teachers should give students assignments that build these skills.

Reading Aloud Complex Informational Texts

Reading aloud builds children's reading comprehension. Let's review some methods teachers can use to incorporate informational texts when reading to students.

When children hear high-quality material being read, their listening and language aptitudes develop. Teachers want to inspire critical thinking in their students, and stopping to ask questions during read alouds can help. Encourage inferential and evaluative comprehension by asking why certain events happened in the texts. After the teacher has asked a few questions, students may feel comfortable enough to ask some of their own.

Engaging students in activities during or after reading sessions can help them understand the content. These activities should be fun! Making art, reenacting scenes, and recreating food related to the texts can be enjoyable for students and teachers. If reading an autobiography, consider projecting an interactive map to point out important locations mentioned by the author.

Workgroups are great for helping students process the texts they read. Putting students into small groups to discuss different parts of an informational story fosters discussion and teamwork. If reading news articles, teachers can ask group members to work together to research and find related stories.

Informational texts are not typically considered exciting reading material, especially textbooks. Using these strategies to teach them makes the process more entertaining. When children are entertained, they are much more likely to absorb the information presented to them.

Scaffolding Comprehension and Analysis of Informational Texts

Chunking is breaking up words into manageable pieces. Scaffolding is similar to chunking in that lessons and texts are divided into sections that are easily digestible by students. Each "scaffold" usually focuses on key areas. This reading comprehension technique is broadly used to help students analyze informational texts.

Create strategic, text-dependent questions in advance. When reading the text in class, stop frequently to discuss a particular section. Ask the section-specific questions that you have prepared. Make sure each question is open-ended to cultivate academic discussion. Give the students some time to talk to each other about the questions.

Being able to annotate and take good notes are skills every student should learn. Provide students an example of what constitutes good notes, like highlighting important words and defining them. Show the students how to organize the notes in an order that makes sense and makes the notes easily accessible. Demonstrate how to write legibly and create memorable abbreviations.

Using semantic maps (graphic organizers) helps visualize and structure concepts from the informational text they have read. They can draw these maps or use PowerPoint to create them. Some common ones are in the form of Venn diagrams and hierarchical organizers. Even a basic outline is an example of a semantic map. These maps not only layout useful parts of the reading, but they also help students complete other assignments, like writing essays about the texts.

Being able to discuss informational texts with their peers is necessary for children's comprehension and social skills. They should be asking each other questions and responding to them. To start them off, pair students up and ask them to come up with text-specific questions for each other. Having engaged them in questioning while reading together earlier, they should have some idea of what questions to create. Still, provide them with a few examples. Tell them to come up with a specific number of queries for their partners (three or so should suffice).

Different Informational Text Structures and Characteristics

Students will encounter the following informational text structures:

- **Descriptive:** describes in great detail.
- **Comparison/contrast:** shows how elements are similar and different. Keywords include "comparable" and "unlike."
- **Cause/effect:** describes the causes and effects that occur in text. Keywords often include "accordingly" and "consequently."
- **Sequential/chronological:** events are presented in order (e.g., beginning, middle, end).

No matter which type of informational text they read, students need to be able to grasp the central ideas and summarize them with supportive evidence. Central ideas are what the overall text is about. Textual features such as headings, bold or italicized text, and bullet points all help students identify the main ideas. Two other features that help students find texts' central ideas are the introductory and closing paragraphs. Often, just reading these two paragraphs is enough to glean what information was presented. This tip is especially helpful for young readers who have a hard time absorbing all of the information in an article, chapter, or other part of the text.

Graphic features, such as charts and diagrams, also provide clues about a text's content. Skimming the material to look for these things is a quick way to figure out a text's primary concepts. Graphic features that are implemented correctly should help students understand a text's overall meaning. When comparing these features to the content itself, especially in a book, they should go hand in hand. To help students learn to compare and contrast the two, have them look over the graphics before reading the text. Ask questions to see if they notice where the graphics represented the text well and where there were key differences, like an important fact being left out.

The characteristics of digital and multimodal texts can often overlap. For example, videos are digital texts. Videos that display closed captioning would be considered multimodal because they feature two modes: visual and written. A book PDF on a website is considered a digital text, whereas a website with interactive graphics would be considered multimodal.

Young readers need to learn how to analyze an author's work by determining their purpose and audience. The first question students need to answer is why an author wrote their content. Was their goal to inform, entertain, or convince? To determine this, tell them to keep the following in mind:

- Informational content usually presents facts.
- Entertaining text typically involves drama or humor.
- Convincing writing often tries to move the audience to think differently or take action.

Remembering these three things can also help students figure out an author's target audience. Understanding the purpose for the writing almost immediately identifies who it was written for.

Help students pick up on the type of language used in a text. Ask what types of descriptions are provided. Are they extremely detailed, wordy, or straight to the point? If the text is informational, what kind of evidence was used to support the main topic?

All readers need to understand the difference between facts and opinions. Tell students to remember this rule of thumb: facts can be verified. This will help build their research skills. Assign them a news article and an opinion piece to compare and contrast.

Finally, teach students to identify the claim in an argumentative text. These texts usually have a thesis and a conclusion; tell students to identify these elements first and then find evidence to support their claims. Have students make a graphic organizer like an essay outline highlighting the thesis, supporting evidence, and conclusion.

Promoting Comprehension of Complex Informational Texts at All Three Comprehension Levels

As previously mentioned, there are three levels of comprehension: literal, inferential, and evaluative. When it comes to reading complex informational texts, teachers should support children's ability to comprehend them, with these levels in mind. Here are some ways.

Start by assigning each student appropriate reading material. For example, if a few students are still reading at levels that are lower or higher than their current grade, provide content at those levels. This is a form of differentiating instruction; each child will read differently, so it is important to cater to the needs of each one.

Simultaneously, teachers should review decoding skills to help bring students up to speed or refresh the skills for advanced readers. This will help prepare them for more complex texts as they are introduced. Frequent reminders of how to decode are always a plus.

Synthesizing simply means collecting and comparing information from more than one source. Give students at least two different texts with similar themes and have them prepare a list of their similarities and differences. This method promotes critical thinking by making the students draw conclusions about each text.

Use this process to encourage students to generate higher-order questions, such as open questions. First, provide them examples of a few higher-order questions and explain their purpose. You may want to create a few questions that address the perspectives that are included from the texts they read. Then, allow them some time to create a few of their own. After they have finished, separate the students into pairs and have them ask each other or swap their lists of questions and answer them independently.

Disciplinary Literacy

Disciplinary literacy focuses on the information and communication tools used within a specific discipline. Texts written about science, math, history, and art are all read and interpreted differently.

Informational texts are good tools for teaching disciplinary literacy. For example, to prepare students to read a science book, teachers can introduce them to scientific articles and other similar reading material. By assigning samples of texts from various disciplines, reading teachers help prepare their students for those classes. In fact, students who learn to read a variety of texts early on tend to outperform their peers who have not been afforded the same instruction. They are also more likely to be active participants in class because they have some familiarity with the material.

Not only do different fields require different reading strategies, but they also have discipline-specific terms. Some of these terms are homographs (words that are spelled the same but have different meanings), like the word *ruler*. In math, a ruler is a measurement tool, but in a historical context, it might refer to a monarch or head of state.

Discipline-specific vocabulary is the third tier of vocabulary, the others being basic (tier one) and academic (tier two). Again, informational texts are useful for instruction. Students will encounter passages in those texts that are unfamiliar and jargon heavy. To help them decipher the content, revisit morphemic analysis and decoding instruction. Picking up on context clues, breaking words down, and defining their morphemes are the most valuable skills a student can have when reading field-specific content. Have students highlight the most difficult terms they encounter and break them down together in class.

Vocabulary and spelling tests will always have their places. They are especially helpful when teaching specific vocabulary because they require students to memorize the terms, which they can then recall as they become applicable in other classes.

Differentiating Instruction in Comprehension and Analysis of Complex Informational Texts

To vary instruction, teachers should do the following: assess each student's learning needs; create a welcoming learning environment built on communication; and allow room for flexibility and modification of content.

To meet the needs of different learners, teachers can modify the informational content that they teach. Group activities, quiet reading time, presentations, and digital resources are all ways to teach the same text in different ways. For example, if the class is reading an autobiographical piece, the teacher can assign an essay writing activity, play audio recordings (like books on tape), and create story maps to teach the overall story.

When reading collectively, ask students to highlight areas of the text they do not understand. Then, open up the classroom to discussion. Allow time for a question-and-answer session.

Ask students how they would like to process the information. Some may prefer to read it individually, while others may need a one-on-one session with the teacher. Others might ask if there are videos online related to the text they are about to read. When it comes to assignments, give them options, like creating artwork or writing journal entries.

Practice Questions

1. Which of the following terms refers to techniques that allow students to progress toward a greater level of understanding on an increasingly independent level?
    a. Discourse
    b. Differentiation
    c. Scaffolding
    d. Benchmarking

2. Which of the following statements about literacy development is true?
    a. Research shows that literacy development begins as early as 3 months of age.
    b. Between 3 and 6 months, babies begin to study a speaker's mouth and listen closely to speech sounds.
    c. Between 6 and 9 months, babies can generally recognize a growing number of commonly repeated words, utter simple words, respond appropriately to simple requests, and begin to attempt to group sounds.
    d. Between 9 and 12 months, babies rapidly strengthen their communication skills, connecting sounds to meanings and combining sounds to create coherent sentences.

3. Receptive language development refers to which of the following stages of literacy?
    a. Beginning literacy
    b. Early intermediate literacy
    c. Intermediate literacy
    d. Early advanced literacy

4. Which of the following is NOT considered a non-decodable sight word?
    a. None
    b. Who
    c. Runner
    d. Said

5. While studying vocabulary, a student notices that the words *circumference*, *circumnavigate*, and *circumstance* all begin with the prefix *circum–*. The student uses her knowledge of affixes to infer that all of these words share what related meaning?
    a. Around, surrounding
    b. Travel, transport
    c. Size, measurement
    d. Area, location

See answers on the next page.

Answer Explanations

1. C: *Scaffolding* refers to techniques that allow students to progress toward a greater level of understanding on an increasingly independent level by incrementally increasing difficulty and independence. *Discourse* is a general term that refers to oral or written communication, so Choice *A* is incorrect. *Differentiation* refers to tailoring instructional methods and activities towards individual students or different levels. Therefore, Choice *B* is incorrect. Choice *D* is incorrect because *benchmarking* refers to setting measurable standards during the learning process.

2. B: Choice *B* is a correct statement about the generally accepted progression of normal literacy development. Choice *A* is incorrect because research indicates that literacy development begins from birth. Choices *C* and *D* are incorrect because those skills start developing a bit later than stated, between 9 and 12 months of age for Choice *C*, and in the toddler years for Choice *D*.

3. A: Receptive language development is a term used to describe the beginning literacy stage, during which children begin understanding the "input" of language. This means that they start developing the ability to connect words with their meanings and comprehend spoken language that others say or read.

4. C: The word *runner* is a decodable word because it follows the rules of phonics and is spelled phonetically. The other three choices are considered non-decodable sight words that students simply need to memorize because they are not spelled phonetically.

5. A: The affix *circum–* originates from Latin and means "around" or "surrounding". It is also related to other words that indicate something round, such as *circle* and *circus*.

Domain IV - Analysis and Response

Analysis and Response

Analyzing, Interpreting, and Discussing the Results of Reading Assessments

Norm-Referenced Assessments
Norm-referenced assessments are formal tests that compare students' scores to state or national averages. They provide each student's score with a percentile, and they can be used to screen struggling students.

Two common norm-referenced assessments are the SAT and ACT. These tests measure students' abilities in reading, writing, and math. They then calculate each student's score as both a number and a percentile.

Criterion-Referenced Assessments
Criterion-referenced assessments may be formal or informal. These tests compare students' skills to predetermined levels of competency and are typically administered multiple times a year to measure student progress.

One example of a criterion-referenced assessment is the **Informal Reading Inventory**. This assessment tests students' abilities to read and understand texts at four levels. The Independent Level is the level of text that a student can read unassisted and comprehend with 90 to 100 percent accuracy. The Instructional Level is the level of text that is best suited for use in the classroom: the student needs a teacher's help to completely understand the passage but can comprehend about 70 to 85 percent of the material. The Hearing Capacity Level is the level of text that the student can comprehend with more than 70 percent accuracy when it is read aloud. Finally, a text at Frustration Level is too difficult; the student's reading comprehension is below 70 percent. Teachers typically use the Informal Reading Inventory at the first of the year to screen for struggling students, then they administer it several times throughout the year to track their students' progress.

Performance-Based Assessments
Performance-based assessments measure a student's ability to apply skills. These assessments require higher-level thinking, not just memorization. For example, students might write an evaluative essay to show that they understand a text.

The essay is a common performance-based assessment. Instead of simply stating the facts they learned in class, students demonstrate their ability to interact with information by creating a compelling argument.

Purposes for Assessments
Screening is a preventative attempt to identify students who are at risk of falling behind grade level. These tests are typically administered at the start of the year with the aim of offering supplemental help to struggling students.

Diagnostic assessments measure specific skills, such as a student's ability to sound out the letter "b." These assessments may be formal exams or informal observations in class.

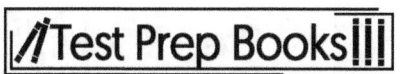

Progress monitoring assessments track student progress during the academic year. These tests may be used only with struggling students, or with the class as a whole. They help teachers learn whether their students have mastered the material and thereby know whether to review or move on.

Outcome assessments (or **high stakes assessments**) take place once a year and are used to assess the teacher and curriculum as well as the students. Staff and parents can compare students' scores and class averages to state or national averages. By doing so, they can determine whether the curriculum and/or teacher are leading to student success.

Identifying Students' Needs Related to Foundational Reading Skills

The best way to identify students' varying needs is to assess their reading on a regular basis.

Note the errors students make when they read and write. Are they including words in sentences that do not belong? Are they inflecting the wrong syllables? Are they leaving out important words that make phrases complete? Spend some time reviewing proper sentence structure in class to help eliminate these issues.

When reading together as a class or one-on-one, encourage slow, deliberate reading aloud. This will enable you to pick up on words that students cannot pronounce properly. Pause after each passage and ask them what the words they just read meant; if they cannot answer clearly, they may be exhibiting decoding difficulties. Take note of whether the students lose their places when reading or have to repeat certain content more than once.

Notice which students are eager to volunteer for reading aloud and which are not. The disengaged students are not necessarily shy. They might have trouble reading fluently or understanding the terms in the text, or they might be unable to pronounce certain words, leading them to lack confidence in their abilities. Do not put these students on the spot; the best tactic would be to pull them aside during quiet reading time and work with them individually to address their needs.

Addressing Students' Needs in Foundational Reading Skills

There are four foundational reading skills: fluency, phonological awareness, print concepts, and phonics/word recognition. Not all students will equally perform each of these skills; some will have a harder time with one or more of them, while others excel. Once a teacher has observed that their students are having a hard time with certain foundational reading skills, they can use a number of best practices to address the issues.

Use structured, clear lessons. Children who are learning English as a second language and those who have learning disabilities benefit tremendously from explicit instruction. Providing students with simple, straightforward, and sequential guidance enables students to catch up to speed with their classmates and work more efficiently on their assignments.

Reliable, high-quality tools are vital parts of classroom instruction. If the material being used to teach children is not up to par, not only will it be more difficult to instruct foundational skills, but doing so could have adverse effects on children's learning. Some students might regress into lower levels of ability and feel incapable of advancement if the quality of their learning tools is low.

Variety is also important, both in terms of the type of instruction and the materials being used. If an educator uses the same tools and teaching methods repeatedly, they risk losing the attention and participation of their students. Lack of variety also leaves many students by the wayside because they do not all learn from the same techniques or materials. Various teaching tools can include videos, graphic organizers, audio recordings, and music, to name a few. Differentiated teaching methods can include individual reading instruction, organizing students into pairs or other small groups, and reading aloud.

It never hurts to revisit the basics of reading. Revisiting the instruction of vowels and syllables, spelling and pronouncing common words, and reintroducing different print concepts are ways to reinforce foundational reading skills. For students still developing phonological awareness skills, being retaught simple phonics might address their lack of knowledge of a certain concept.

Selecting Instructional Strategies to Address Students' Needs

Identify the goals for each reading lesson before teaching them, then modify instruction accordingly. Students' foundational reading needs cannot be addressed in the exact same way, so varying instruction is necessary. Using a multimodal approach is best.

The presentation of reading content is important. Hands-on learning activities improve children's learning experiences while addressing their skill levels. Such activities include building vocabulary words with blocks, using slideshows to present images or recreate scenes, and playing sight-word Twister. Sight-word Twister is attaching words to the different colors of the Twister mat and playing accordingly.

Providing regular feedback is an intervention strategy. Do not just point out the areas where students are struggling with reading assignments; tell them when they have done well, too. Start with a positive before constructively pointing out errors in reading or writing.

Reading the same passage multiple times is an example of Fluency-Oriented Reading Instruction (FORI). This strategy entails not only reading the same thing repeatedly, but doing so in different ways. This makes it interesting for the students while also addressing fluency needs. Echo reading, partner reading, and reading aloud are a few ways to implement FORI. Playing games centered around the text, giving mini tests, and creating other projects around the content are also encouraged.

Students whose foundational reading needs are not addressed early enough reportedly exhibit poor academic performance. By using intervention and instructional strategies, teachers help prevent this from happening.

Significant Student Needs Related to Reading Comprehension

Vocabulary Knowledge
Students with learning disabilities and those who speak English as a second language often struggle with vocabulary. This will be evident when they are reading out loud in class, as they may pause when they approach certain words, skip them entirely, or struggle when trying to pronounce them. These students may also exhibit poor oral language skills.

To help, teachers should take note of the words students struggle with, then regularly pronounce and define them in class. Assign vocabulary worksheets with commonly misunderstood words on a regular basis so that students have to select or write in the correct definitions. Provide plenty of examples of how the words should be properly used.

Knowledge of Sentence Structures

Many students have trouble with sentence structure. This will be most evident in their written assignments. Give them plenty of opportunities to write essays or fill in answers on text-relevant worksheets.

Provide explicit instruction of the four types of sentences: simple, compound, complex, and compound-complex. Write sentences on the board or provide word maps that identify the various parts of sentences to students. Diagramming sentences is an old school technique that teachers can always rely on to teach sentence structure. Make sure students have plenty of opportunities to practice diagramming on their own.

Application of Comprehension Skills

The number one sign that a child may not be comprehending text is a lack of interest or engagement. When questioned about the meanings of the texts, these children may struggle to provide coherent answers. They could also become fixated on or simply omit crucial elements of the content.

Again, teaching vocabulary and spending time teaching children how to identify context clues is important here. Use graphic organizers to assist with this instruction. Consider areas where your instruction strategies can be adjusted.

Analysis of Literary or Informational Texts

Analyzing texts is hard; even advanced readers struggle with it. A sign of this difficulty is a student unable to identify the main concept of a piece of writing. This child may have had a hard time learning to decode in the first place. When doling out assignments, notice if the student is providing thorough, detailed answers or some that could use more information.

Students can become better at analysis by learning to gather textual evidence. If they are given leading questions that point to context clues, it will be easier for them to identify important information in the texts. In literary texts, remind them to identify the main characters, plot, and settings; then ask them specific questions about what happened with each. For informational texts, teach them how to read the thesis statement, conclusion, and supporting images.

Peer-Assisted Learning Strategies

As discussed earlier, there are a number of intervention strategies to address students' reading comprehension needs. Let's take a closer look at one of them.

Peer-Assisted Learning Strategies (PALS) pair an underperforming reader with a stronger one. The concept was created by Vanderbilt University scholars. Countless studies have since shown that using PALS is one of the best ways to address reading comprehension.

Once two students are paired, they take turns reading and reciting texts to one another. The stronger reader provides the other student with constant feedback that helps them improve. Implementing PALS in addition to face-to-face reading with the instructor has proven to help English learners and students with diverse learning profiles.

PALS, in particular, is more effective than normal workgroups where there are three or more students learning together. Children usually respond better to an audience of one; they feel less intimidated and encouraged to keep reading.

PALS is not exclusive to reading classes. Instructors in other topics like math, music, and science also benefit from putting students into pairs to study together.

This form of peer teaching does more than just encourage children to read. Peer learners will become more confident in their abilities, not just in reading, but other academic areas.

Teachers can also differentiate instruction using PALS by assigning unique activities to each pair of students. They will have observed the learning styles of the students beforehand, so it is wise to take advantage of this opportunity by introducing new, tailored projects.

Most importantly, PALS should be fun. Give students a few different types of reading material to enjoy and encourage them to play games that involve the text. Notice the changes in the students' behavior when they work with their peers. If it is not an enjoyable experience for them, switch gears and use a new strategy.

Explaining the Effectiveness of Selected Instructional Strategies

Teachers' methods of instruction are frequently evaluated. At some point, you will need to provide the rationale for implementing certain instructional strategies to address students' comprehension needs. Luckily, there is plenty of data to support these methods.

The purpose of instructional intervention is to make students confident enough to become individual readers. The right strategies help teachers monitor and maintain a record of students' progress, teach students how to properly organize information, and spark student interest in the classroom.

Instructional strategies foster meaningful connections between students, their peers, and the instructors. They include explicit instructions that make information more digestible to young learners. Intervention introduces students to a plethora of high-quality, informative, and entertaining texts that broaden their knowledge. They also immerse children in cooperative learning environments.

These methods make independent learners who are able to assess their own reading progress. The skills children learn from instructional reading strategies are largely transferrable to other classrooms and topics. They are also noted to improve children's overall cognitive functions.

Practice Questions

1. Roger has been teaching his kindergarten class new words and story structure. He uses poems and music that are focused on characters having adventures. The stories often rhyme, and the children in his class thoroughly enjoy them. What type of story is Roger using to teach his class?
    a. Myths
    b. Fairy tales
    c. Nursery rhymes
    d. Folklore

2. Mary has been reading stories aloud to her first-grade class, but she notices that some students are not as interested. She wants to have the students do some sort of activity that will be fun and encourage them to speak up. Which of the following activities would be a good way for Mary to engage her students?
    a. Use hand puppets to represent the characters in the stories while she reads.
    b. Take the students outside for a brief recess.
    c. Stop for quiet, individual reading time.
    d. Show the students a movie.

3. Teachers are asked to keep records of students' learning progress throughout the school year. Of the options below, which would be the most helpful for recording data?
    a. Notebooks
    b. Spreadsheets
    c. Report cards
    d. Word document

4. Describe the inferential reading comprehension level.
    a. It is what the reader can actually see, hear, or read.
    b. The reader draws conclusions from context clues.
    c. The reader hypothesizes what the text means.
    d. It is when the reader has a personal reaction to the text.

5. What is scaffolding?
    a. Breaking words down into parts
    b. Dividing words into syllables
    c. Analyzing individual morphemes
    d. Dividing texts into digestible sections

See answers on the next page.

Answer Explanations

1. C: Nursery rhymes are poems or songs that teach children new terms and stories. Choice *A* is incorrect; myths are stories told to attempt to explain the origin of something. Choice *B* is incorrect because while fairy tales can be as entertaining as nursery rhymes, they are not sung; they are short stories that sometimes contain supernatural elements. Choice *D* is incorrect because folklore are orated stories about common people.

2. A: The best way for Mary to keep her students engaged would be to use hand puppets as a supplement; this activity may spark greater engagement from both visual and kinesthetic learners. Stopping for a recess may be a good idea for a break, but it will not encourage students to engage when they get back. Stopping for individual reading time will not encourage the students to speak up and may further isolate them from engaging. Showing the students a movie might be fun, but it is more of a passive activity and will not engage students in the way Mary wants.

3. B: It is recommended that teachers keep spreadsheets to track students' progress in grades and skill development. While the other tools could be used for keeping track of data, they are not the best options. Notebooks and Word documents do not organize information as efficiently as spreadsheets, and report cards are primarily tools for students and parents (not teachers) to stay informed about the students' progress.

4. B: The inferential reading comprehension level is when the reader draws conclusions from context clues in the text. Choice *A* describes literal reading comprehension. Choice *C* describes evaluative reading comprehension. Choice *D* does not describe a type of reading comprehension.

5. D: Scaffolding is breaking texts down into sections and dissecting their key points. Breaking words down into parts and analyzing individual morphemes are both parts of morphology. Dividing words into syllables is syllabication.

Writing Strategies for Constructed Responses

When preparing for the constructed response section of the test, it is important to identify what the scenario is asking you to analyze and to make sure that your ideas are organized. Typically, a constructed response question will give you a scenario to analyze. The scenario will pertain to the science of teaching reading. Additionally, the question will include the information it wants you to specifically address in your response, as well as some additional information that could assist you in constructing your response. When writing for this portion of the test, you should keep in mind what qualifies as effective composition and effective written expression. Planning and organizing your ideas before writing your response, along with understanding what makes for *good* writing, will help you to succeed in this section.

Effective Composing

Good writing is composed of several key elements: development, focus, clarity and coherence, grammatical proficiency, and originality. Different institutions and individual instructors will list such qualities differently, but good composition will have these basic qualities.

Strong compositions have well-developed ideas that are explained clearly throughout the piece. Good writing seems to have been planned and executed without any gaps or confusion. Through their writing, students must essentially develop an idea and line of reasoning that leave readers clear about the focus of the piece. This also means that paragraphs must be arranged in a way that they enhance and expand on the central focus of the paper, using evidence sensibly.

A writer's focus is the central point. A successful composition will not only contain a clear focus but carry the focus throughout the piece. The reader should never lose the focus or be confused by it. The way in which the content is presented throughout the text, while remaining focused on the central idea, is key. This is done by the tactical use of evidence surrounding and supporting claims relating to the central idea.

Language can be elegant and creative, but it must be used in a way the reader can understand. Much of a writer's success will depend on the coherence of the written piece. Paragraphs and the ideas within them should not be random but connect together, seamlessly blending into the next section to advance the focus of the writing. Each paragraph should strengthen the claim. Unnecessary paragraphs disrupt the flow of the writing and distract the reader, ultimately weakening the piece. Naturally, the writing should also be grammatically correct and proofed for accurate spelling and sentence structure.

Originality is the defining aspect of a well-written piece. Students should not parrot the writing style or ideas of others but instead write something that is unique. Ideas, and the way they are presented, should be fresh and approach topics in a way that offers a new perspective to the reader.

Effective Written Expression

Written expression refers to the ability of the writer to fluidly communicate meaning and purpose throughout the composition. Essentially, this refers not only to how clear the central focus of the piece is but how well the ideas surrounding the central focus are presented. If the writer can't successfully express the meaning and implications of the idea, the writing will not be strong.

Effective written expression utilizes detailed, clear communication. A writer doesn't need to unload elaborate diction throughout the paragraphs. Such an embellishment can be distracting to the reader, which actually defeats the principles behind effective writing. Sentences should be direct and emphasize language that, while engaging, remains simple enough for the audience to understand. This doesn't mean abstaining from using advanced words but rather keeping sentences direct and to the point. Students should avoid rambling line after line. Avoiding exaggerating language or overdramatic phrasing is also important. Not only can this confuse the reader, it can also harm the reader's credibility.

A simple formula for effective writing is to introduce an idea, discuss it, and then make a conclusion. This applies for the written piece as a whole but must also be used within individual paragraphs. If a writer just introduces idea after idea with no substance, the reader is left with unsubstantiated claims. Without supporting evidence to understand the view, the reader is left with only opinion. With the implementation of facts and supporting details, this opinion is strengthened. Thus, the reasoning behind the central idea is clearly executed and can be considered seriously. This helps the writer achieve credibility.

Paragraph coherence is vital for effective written expression. Paragraph sequencing and information placement are essential to streamlining the entire piece. Evidence and supporting information should be used to transition from one section to another, up to the conclusion. This enables the information to be clearly expressed. The author should strive to write in a way that, as the piece progresses, the focus becomes clearer and more convincing. By the conclusion of the written piece, the author should also restate their thesis to solidify their views and reasoning.

Practice Test

Reading Pedagogy

1. Carson wants to improve his students' metacognition. What would be a good step for him to take?
    I. Asking students why they think what they think
    II. Always telling his students whether their ideas are correct or incorrect
    III. Encouraging students to think about their own learning styles and use study techniques that work for them
    IV. Allowing his students to choose books that interest them
    a. I and II
    b. II and III
    c. I and III
    d. II and IV

2. What is a fallacy?
    a. A misuse of logic
    b. A false conclusion to a logical argument
    c. An incorrect fact
    d. A sign that a source is not reliable

3. What is the difference between a discussion circle and a debate?
    a. A discussion has no "right" or "wrong" side, whereas a debate does.
    b. A discussion is more formal than a debate.
    c. A debate breaks the students into two teams, whereas a discussion circle is a single group.
    d. A debate harms a student's sense of community, whereas a discussion builds community.

4. Why is annotation a beneficial exercise for students?
    a. It teaches them to think independently.
    b. It helps them learn to identify key points.
    c. It teaches them to write faster.
    d. It helps shy students engage in discussion.

5. Which of the following is a stakeholder in a school?
    I. A parent
    II. A school administrator
    III. A teacher
    IV. A school board member
    a. I and II
    b. I and III
    c. I, II, and III
    d. All of the above

6. Martine wants to increase her students' caregiver involvement. Which measure should she implement?
    a. Giving students homework assignments to be completed with their caregiver
    b. Asking caregivers to read aloud at home
    c. Loaning out materials from the classroom
    d. Inviting caregivers into the classroom

7. Which statement about choosing a reading program for learner-centered education is true?
    a. Use older materials because they have been tested by numerous teachers.
    b. Use a program that offers options so that you can tailor the program to your students.
    c. Never blend two programs, as it makes things confusing for the students.
    d. Use the program that the other teachers in your school are using.

8. Jasmine wants to improve her reading program. In which order should she proceed?
    a. Assess students, modify the program, identify weaknesses, experiment with different techniques, reassess students.
    b. Modify the program, assess students, identify weaknesses, reassess students, experiment with different techniques.
    c. Assess students, identify weaknesses, modify the program, experiment with different techniques, reassess students.
    d. Experiment with different techniques, assess students, modify the program, identify weaknesses, reassess students.

9. What is the role of a paraprofessional?
    a. To teach lessons independently
    b. To design the curriculum
    c. To manage class behavior and support learning
    d. To tutor struggling children outside of class

10. Which task should a teacher assign to their teaching aide?
    a. Planning lessons
    b. Teaching a class
    c. Working with struggling students
    d. Writing tests and quizzes

11. What kind of assessment is most beneficial for a student with a diverse literacy profile?
    a. Frequent and ongoing
    b. Weekly
    c. Monthly
    d. Summative assessments only at the end of a unit of study

12. Laura plans to test her students at the first of the year. She wants to assess specific skills to find out if students have any weaknesses that they need to work on. Which kind of assessment should Laura use?
    a. Screening assessment
    b. Diagnostic assessment
    c. Progress monitoring assessment
    d. Outcomes assessment

Practice Test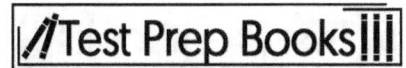

Reading Development: Foundational Skills

1. What is the spelling stage of a student who looks at a word and is able to tell the teacher that the letters spell C-A-T, but who cannot actually say the word?
    a. Alphabetic Spelling
    b. Within Word Pattern Spelling
    c. Derivational Relations Spelling
    d. Emergent Spelling

2. Predicting, summarizing, questioning, and clarifying are steps of what?
    a. Reciprocal teaching
    b. Comprehensive teaching
    c. Activation teaching
    d. Summative teaching

3. What are students utilizing when they ask themselves, *What do I know?*, *What do I want to know?*, and *What have I learned?* and record the answers in a table?
    a. Self-monitoring comprehension
    b. KWL charts
    c. Metacognitive skills
    d. Directed reading-thinking activities

4. What technique might an author use to let the reader know that the main character was in a car crash as a child?
    a. Point of view
    b. Characterization
    c. Figurative language
    d. Flashback

5. A graphic organizer is a method of achieving what?
    a. Integrating knowledge and ideas
    b. Generating questions
    c. Determining point of view
    d. Determining the author's purpose

6. A student is trying to decide if a character is telling the truth about having stolen candy. After the student reads that the character is playing with an empty candy wrapper in her pocket, the student decides the character is guilty. This is an example of what?
    a. Flashback
    b. Making an inference
    c. Style
    d. Figurative language

7. What is the method of categorizing text by its structure and literary elements called?
    a. Fiction
    b. Nonfiction
    c. Genre
    d. Plot

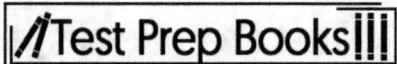

8. A reader is distracted from following a story because he is having trouble understanding why a character decided to cut school. He jumps to the next page to find out where the character is headed. This is an example of what?
    a. Self-monitoring comprehension
    b. KWL charts
    c. Metacognitive skills
    d. Directed reading-thinking activities

9. Which of the following is the best way to utilize a reading center or corner in a classroom?
    a. As a spot for students to play games
    b. As a private and quiet place to chat about books
    c. As a location to provide reading options above students' reading level
    d. As a place for students to take a break from the rigors of the classroom

10. Which trait is most commonly associated with giving individuality and style to writing?
    a. Voice
    b. Word choice
    c. Presentation
    d. Ideas

11. What types of questions should be offered in an assessment in order to check for its validity?
    a. Open-ended questions only
    b. Selected-response questions
    c. Both open-ended questions and multiple-choice questions
    d. None of these

12. In the 6+1 Traits model, which trait ultimately forms the content of the writing?
    a. Conventions
    b. Word choice
    c. Ideas
    d. Voice

13. In the word *shut*, the *sh* is an example of what?
    a. Consonant digraph
    b. Sound segmentation
    c. Vowel digraph
    d. Rime

14. When students identify the phonemes in spoken words, they are practicing which of the following?
    a. Sound blending
    b. Substitution
    c. Rhyming
    d. Segmentation

15. What is the alphabetic principle?
    a. The understanding that letters represent sounds in words
    b. The ability to combine letters to correctly spell words
    c. The proper use of punctuation within writing
    d. The memorization of all the letters in the alphabet

16. Print awareness includes all except which of the following concepts?
    a. The differentiation of uppercase and lowercase letters
    b. The identification of word boundaries
    c. The proper tracking of words
    d. The spelling of sight words

17. When teachers point to words during shared readings, what are they modeling?
    I. Word boundaries
    II. Directionality
    III. One-to-one correspondence
    a. I and II
    b. I and III
    c. II and III
    d. I, II, and III

18. Structural analysis would be the most appropriate strategy in determining the meaning of which of the following words?
    a. Extra
    b. Improbable
    c. Likely
    d. Wonder

19. A student spells *eagle* as *EGL*. This student is performing at which stage of spelling?
    a. Conventional
    b. Phonetic
    c. Semiphonetic
    d. Transitional

20. Spelling instruction should include which of the following?
    I. Word walls
    II. Daily reading opportunities
    III. Daily writing opportunities
    IV. Weekly spelling inventories with words students have studied during the week
    a. I and IV
    b. I, II, and III
    c. I, II, and IV
    d. I, II, III, and IV

21. A kindergarten student is having difficulty distinguishing the letters *b* and *d*. The teacher should do which of the following?
    a. Have the student verbalize the directions of the shapes used when writing each letter.
    b. Have the student identify the letters within grade-appropriate texts.
    c. Have the student write each letter five times.
    d. Have the student write a sentence in which all of the letters start with either *b* or *d*.

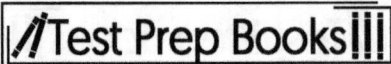

22. When differentiating phonics instruction for English learners (ELs), teachers should do which of the following?
    a. Increase the rate of instruction.
    b. Begin with the identification of word boundaries.
    c. Focus on syllabication.
    d. Help transfer relevant skills from their original language(s).

23. Which of the following is the most appropriate assessment of spelling for students who are performing at the pre-phonetic stage?
    a. Sight word drills
    b. Phonemic awareness tests
    c. Writing samples
    d. Concepts about print (CAP) test

24. Phonological awareness is best assessed through which of the following?
    a. Identification of rimes or onsets within words
    b. Identification of letter-sound correspondences
    c. Comprehension of an audio book
    d. Writing samples

25. The identification of morphemes within words occurs during the instruction of what?
    a. Structural analysis
    b. Syllabic analysis
    c. Phonics
    d. The alphabetic principle

26. Which of the following pairs of words are homophones?
    a. Playful and replay
    b. To and too
    c. Was and were
    d. Gloomy and sad

27. Nursery rhymes are used in kindergarten to develop what?
    a. Print awareness
    b. Phoneme recognition
    c. Syllabication
    d. Structural analysis

28. High-frequency words such as *be, the*, and *or* are taught during the instruction of what?
    a. Phonics skills
    b. Sight word recognition
    c. Vocabulary development
    d. Structural analysis

Practice Test

29. To thoroughly assess students' phonics skills, teachers should administer assessments that require students to do which of the following?
    a. Decode in context only
    b. Decode in isolation only
    c. Both A and B
    d. Neither A nor B

30. A student is having difficulty pronouncing a word that she comes across when reading aloud. Which of the following is most likely NOT a reason for the difficulty that the student is experiencing?
    a. Poor word recognition
    b. A lack of content vocabulary
    c. Inadequate background knowledge
    d. Repeated readings

31. Which is the largest contributor to the development of students' written vocabulary?
    a. Reading
    b. Directed reading
    c. Direct teaching
    d. Modeling

32. The study of roots, suffixes, and prefixes is called what?
    a. Listening comprehension
    b. Word consciousness
    c. Word morphology
    d. Textual analysis

33. Phonemic awareness, phonics, fluency, vocabulary, and comprehension are the five basic elements of what?
    a. Bloom's Taxonomy
    b. Spelling instruction
    c. Reading education
    d. Genre

34. A child reads the story "Little Red Riding Hood" aloud. He easily pronounces the words, uses an apprehensive tone to show that the main character should not be leaving the path, adds a scary voice for the Big Bad Wolf, and reads the story at a pace that engages the class. What are these promising signs of?
    a. Reading fluency
    b. Phonemic awareness
    c. Reading comprehension
    d. Working memory

35. A student is trying to read the word *preferred*. She first recognizes the word *red* at the end, then sounds out the rest of the word by breaking it down into *pre*, then *fer*, then *red*. Finally, she puts it together and says *preferred*. This student is displaying what attribute?
    a. Phonemic awareness
    b. Phonics
    c. Fluency
    d. Vocabulary

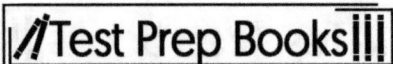

36. A class silently reads a passage on the American Revolution. Once they are done, the teacher asks the students to name the two sides who were fighting, the reason they were fighting, and the winner. What skill is the teacher gauging?
    a. Orthographic development
    b. Fluency
    c. Comprehension
    d. Phonics

37. What is a phoneme?
    a. A word
    b. A relationship between a letter and a sound
    c. An individual sound
    d. A consonant

38. What is the study of what words mean in certain situations?
    a. Morphology
    b. Pragmatics
    c. Syntax
    d. Semantics

Reading Development: Comprehension

1. Which of the following is an essential component of effective reading comprehension?
    a. Reading rate
    b. Genre of text
    c. Size of print
    d. Background knowledge

2. Which of the following is an essential component of effective fluency instruction?
    a. Spelling
    b. Writing
    c. Testing
    d. Practice

3. The Directed Reading Thinking Activity (DRTA) method helps students to do what?
    a. Build prior knowledge by exploring audiovisual resources before a reading
    b. Predict what will occur in a text and search the text to verify the predictions
    c. Identify, define, and review unfamiliar terms
    d. Understand the format of multiple types and genres of text

4. A teacher assigns a writing prompt in order to assess her students' reading skills. Which of the following can be said about this form of reading assessment?
    a. It is the most beneficial way to assess reading comprehension.
    b. It is invalid because a student's ability to read and write are unrelated.
    c. It is erroneous since the strength of a student's reading and writing vocabulary may differ.
    d. It is the worst way to assess reading comprehension.

Practice Test

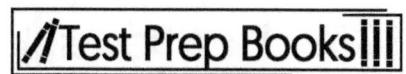

5. When does scaffolded reading occur?
   a. A student hears a recording of herself reading a text in order to set personal reading goals.
   b. A student receives assistance and feedback on strategies to utilize while reading.
   c. A student is given extra time to find the answers to predetermined questions.
   d. A student is pulled out of a class to receive services elsewhere.

6. What are the three interconnected indicators of reading fluency?
   a. Phonetics, word morphology, and listening comprehension
   b. Accuracy, rate, and prosody
   c. Syntax, semantics, and vocabulary
   d. Word exposure, phonetics, and decodable skills

7. Which of the following about effective independent reading is NOT true?
   a. Students should read texts that are below their reading levels during independent reading.
   b. Students need to demonstrate fluency before reading independently.
   c. Students who do not yet display automaticity should whisper to themselves when reading aloud.
   d. Students who demonstrate automaticity in decoding should be held accountable during independent reading.

8. Timed oral reading can be used to assess which of the following?
   a. Phonics
   b. Listening comprehension
   c. Reading rate
   d. Background knowledge

9. Syntax is best described as what?
   a. The arrangement of words into sentences
   b. The study of language meaning
   c. The study of grammar and language structure
   d. The proper formatting of a written text

10. What do informal reading assessments allow that standardized reading assessments do NOT allow?
    a. The application of grade-level norms toward a student's reading proficiency
    b. The personalization of reading assessments in order to differentiate instruction
    c. The avoidance of partialities in the interpretation of reading assessments
    d. The comparison of an individual's reading performance to that of other students in the class

11. When building a class library, a teacher should be cognizant of the importance of what?
    a. Providing fiction that contains concepts relating to the background knowledge of all students in the class.
    b. Utilizing only nonfiction text that correlates to state and national standards in order to reinforce academic concept knowledge.
    c. Utilizing a single genre of text in order to reduce confusion of written structures.
    d. Including a wide range of fiction and nonfiction texts at multiple reading levels.

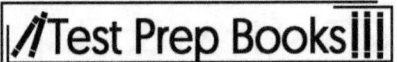

12. Samantha is in second grade and struggles with fluency. Which of the following strategies is likely to be most effective in improving Samantha's reading fluency?
    a. The teacher prompts Samantha when she pauses upon coming across an unknown word.
    b. The teacher records Samantha as she reads aloud.
    c. The teacher reads a passage out loud several times to Samantha and then has Samantha read the same passage.
    d. The teacher uses read-alouds and verbalizes contextual strategies that can be used to identify unfamiliar words.

13. Reading fluency is best described as the ability to do what?
    a. Read smoothly and accurately
    b. Comprehend what is read
    c. Demonstrate phonetic awareness
    d. Properly pronounce a list of words

14. Poetry is often an effective device when teaching what skill?
    a. Fluency
    b. Spelling
    c. Writing
    d. Word decoding

15. A teacher needs to assess students' accuracy in reading high frequency sight words and irregular sight words that are grade-appropriate. Which of the following strategies would be most appropriate for this purpose?
    a. The teacher gives students a list of words to study for a spelling test that will be administered the following week.
    b. The teacher allows students to bring their favorite books from home and has them read their selected text aloud independently.
    c. The teacher administers the Stanford structural analysis assessment to determine students' rote memory and application of morphemes contained within the words.
    d. The teacher records how many words each student reads correctly when reading aloud a list of a teacher-selected, grade-appropriate words.

16. What type of texts are considered nonfiction?
    a. Folktales
    b. Memoirs
    c. Fables
    d. Short stories

17. What is a summative assessment?
    a. A formal assessment that is given at the end of a unit of study
    b. An informal assessment that is given at the end of a unit of study
    c. An assessment that is given daily and is usually only a few questions in length
    d. An assessment given at the end of the week that is usually based on observation

Practice Test

18. How are typographic features useful when teaching reading comprehension?
    a. Typographic features are graphics used to illustrate the story and help students visualize the text.
    b. Typographic features give the answers in boldfaced print.
    c. Typographic features are not helpful when teaching reading comprehension.
    d. Typographic features are used to display changes in topics or to highlight important content.

19. What do English learners need to identify prior to comprehending text?
    a. Vocabulary
    b. Figurative language
    c. Author's purpose
    d. Setting

20. Which of the following is an indication of a reliable source?
    a. Written by a scholar
    b. Found on the internet
    c. Unbiased perspective
    d. Published many years ago

21. What is Freytag's pyramid?
    a. A way of structuring goals for the class
    b. A way of organizing class time
    c. A way of mapping the plot of a story
    d. A way of mapping the relationships between characters in a story

22. Which of the following are necessary criteria for a multicultural text?
    I. The text depicts cultural differences accurately.
    II. The text models positive interactions and engages with social issues.
    III. The text introduces only one new culture at a time.
    IV. The text reflects the diversity in your classroom and community.
    a. I and II
    b. I, II, and III
    c. I, II, and IV
    d. All of the above

Analysis and Response

1. Jennifer is a third grade reading teacher. This semester, she is teaching her students to recognize story structure. Jennifer would like to teach the students to organize the parts of a story visually. Which of the following would be the most appropriate tool to do this?
    a. Online website
    b. Letter tiles
    c. Story map
    d. Word search

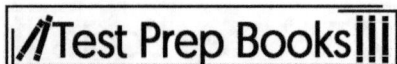

2. Michael is trying to figure out if and how well the students in his kindergarten class can read. He wants to conduct an assessment that will reveal if the children have basic familiarity with common words, syllables, and sounds. What type of assessment should Michael conduct for this purpose?
   a. Pop quizzes
   b. Diagnostic reading assessment
   c. Norm-referenced assessment
   d. Recitation

3. Some first graders are learning about different word parts using letter tiles. In particular, they are learning to break words down and identify their roots, which cannot be divided further. Which parts of words are the children most likely learning about?
   a. Morphemes
   b. Prosody
   c. Semantics
   d. Inflectional suffixes

4. Rebecca has introduced her students to various genres of stories this year. Currently, she is reading stories that include anthropomorphic animals that are faced with serious decisions. Even though the stories center around animals, they share relatable experiences. After she reads each one, Rebecca asks her students what the stories were trying to teach. What kind of story is Rebecca reading to the students?
   a. Tall tales
   b. Fairy tales
   c. Legends
   d. Fables

5. A group of four first graders is learning to read. They know their alphabet and recognize hundreds of words; however, they still need to practice sounding many of them out. Their teacher is working with them to develop their decoding skills. The teacher spends a lot of time teaching these students how to pronounce words correctly and recognize the structure of stories. Based on this information, at what stage of reading development are these four students likely to be in?
   a. Intermediate
   b. Emergent
   c. Beginning
   d. Transitional

6. There are three key assessment concepts: validity, reliability, and equity. Which statement below best describes reliability?
   a. Students' knowledge is assessed on the same scale.
   b. The assessment thoroughly covers the topic at hand and is reputable.
   c. The assessment consistently and adequately analyzes a subject with appropriate material.
   d. Students are graded on various scales.

Practice Test

7. Which of the options below best describes norm-referenced tests?
   a. Students are scored in percentiles and ranked against national averages for others in their age group.
   b. Results are compared to proposed standards of what children should learn by a certain grade.
   c. Test results represent students' knowledge levels as below basic, basic, proficient, or advanced.
   d. Students' knowledge is compared to others in different grade levels.

8. Amanda has been teaching her students the relationships between letters, their sounds, and the words they form. What concept is Amanda teaching her students?
   a. Print concepts
   b. The alphabetic principle
   c. Semantics
   d. Morphemic awareness

9. Which of the following describes the kinesthetic learning style?
   a. Responds to different types of images, including videos, photographs, graphics, and maps.
   b. Absorbs information through lectures, conversations, and reading aloud.
   c. Learn best by writing information or reading text.
   d. Requires immersion and hands-on experiences to retain information.

10. Which option below *best* describes patterned books?
    a. Provides a nonfiction account of a real person's life.
    b. Full of magical characters in imaginary settings.
    c. Presents factual information meant to educate students on particular topics.
    d. Employs visuals and the use of repetition to tell stories.

11. Ian is teaching his students words that sound different and have different meanings but are spelled the same. What are these words called?
    a. Contractions
    b. Homophones
    c. Homographs
    d. Determiners

12. At an early age, children develop phonological awareness. When they begin reading, they learn how to break words down into parts. To teach this, instructors integrate morphemic analysis into their curriculums. Which choice below correctly defines morphemic analysis?
    a. Dividing words into roots, suffixes, and prefixes and figuring out their meanings
    b. Breaking words down into syllables
    c. Interpreting letter-sound relationships
    d. Recognizing the patterns in words

13. There are four types of bound morphemes: derivational, inflectional, contracted forms, and bound bases. Which morphemes below represent inflectional morphemes?
    a. 'll, 're, 'ive
    b. -ing, -est, -'s
    c. cran-, -sent, -mit
    d. pre-, un-, -ful

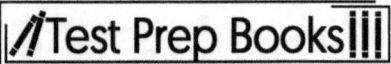

14. Which of the following is NOT an example of an uncommon vowel type?
    a. Schwa
    b. Consonant-le
    c. Open
    d. Copula

15. Tanya has a student who speaks English as a second language. This student is struggling with syllabication. Which intervention strategy listed below would be the most appropriate to address this student's needs?
    a. Repeatedly recite the words
    b. Group students in pairs and provide reading assignments
    c. Frequently administer spelling tests
    d. Identify vowels and division patterns

16. PALS are strategies that pair students into tutor/tutee collaborations to help struggling readers. What does PALS stand for?
    a. Pair Arranged Learning Style
    b. Peer-Assisted Learning Strategies
    c. Partner-Assisted Learning Strategy
    d. Peer-Arranged Learning Solution

17. There are three levels of reading comprehension. What are they?
    a. Literal, inferential, evaluative
    b. Adequate, influential, evaluating
    c. Emulative, adequate, literal
    d. Inferential, contemplative, evaluative

18. Carey uses a lot of imagery in her reading classes. Her favorite tool organizes stories into a palatable format that often uses images, word bubbles, and outlines. It can also be used to break stories down into hierarchies. What type of learning tool is Carey using?
    a. Slideshow
    b. Word tiles
    c. Graphic organizer
    d. Patterned book

Constructed Response

Directions: Provide an in-depth written response to the question provided. Be sure to plan and organize your response before you write it. You may use citations, but you may not copy or paraphrase anyone else's work.

Assignment

Use the information in the scenario below to write a reply in which you use your understanding of literacy assessment and instructional strategies to examine this case study. Your response should completely address the following in 400-600 words:

- Identify a need the student has that may indicate a learning disorder.

- Describe an effective instructional strategy that would address the need of the student related to the identified learning disorder.

- Describe some teaching strategies that can be used to help the student improve.

- Explain why each of your instructional strategies would be effective in helping the student's needs related to reading standards as described in the TEKS for ELAR.

Scenario

Scenario: The following case study is focused on Caleb, a second grade student. Caleb's primary instructor has noticed that when Caleb reads material aloud in class, he will often take long pauses and read the sentences slower than the other students. This sometimes causes him to stutter or hesitate during longer sentences. Another issue is that sometimes he will switch the order of the words he sees, for example, putting the word *the* after the word *cat* in a sentence. Despite this, Caleb is very bright and seems to fully grasp the context of the material. He also appears to be engaged when answering questions but is hesitant when having to read in front of the class. Caleb's teacher has requested that Mr. Breiner, the reading specialist, evaluate Caleb to understand what might be causing his issues. While Caleb is highly intelligent, the teacher is wondering whether his problems with reading may indicate a diverse learning profile. Mr. Breiner has been requested to present ideas on how to help Caleb's reading skills improve. The teacher wants to be able to learn how to address reading issues like Caleb's in the future, or at least be able to identify core literary issues very early in the developmental stage.

Teacher Notes

- When reading the sentence, "The next-door neighbors adopted the cat that had been homeless," Caleb switched *the* and *cat*. He also seemed to take longer to sound out *homeless*.

- Longer sentences seem to cause Caleb confusion when reading aloud.

- In some of his writing responses, Caleb will sometimes switch the letters within the words or the words themselves.

- Caleb understands material clearly and gives insightful thoughts aloud. No speech problems were observed.

Answer Explanations

Reading Pedagogy

1. C: Metacognition is the ability to think about one's thoughts. Asking students why they think what they think, option *I*, improves metacognition by compelling students to examine their thoughts. Encouraging students to think about their learning style, option *III*, also hones metacognition. Always correcting or praising students' ideas, option *II*, does not contribute to metacognition because it encourages students to think there is just one right answer. Allowing students to choose their own books, option *IV*, is a way of sparking student engagement, not fostering metacognition.

2. A: Fallacies are invalid logical processes. For example, consider the following argument: "Sam is an animal. He is not a cat, so he must be a dog." This is a fallacy because cats and dogs are not the only two animals. Choices *B* and *C* refer to the claim rather than the thought process. Choice *D* refers to criteria for evaluating sources.

3. C: Debates are built on two conflicting views, whereas discussion circles enable students to express their personal opinions; there might be as many opinions in the circle as there are students. Choice *A* is not necessarily true. Many issues and topics of morality, principles, ethics, and ideals are both discussed and debated, and there is often no clear "right" or "wrong" side. Choice *B* is false because debates typically require more formal preparation than discussions. Choice *D* is untrue, as classroom debates can be fun activities that also foster a sense of community.

4. B: Annotating texts teaches students to determine what information is important. Choices *A* and *C* may be true in some cases, but they are not necessarily related to annotation. Choice *D* is false because annotating does not involve class discussion.

5. D: A stakeholder in a school is anyone who has a vested interest in the school. Parents, school administrators, teachers, and school board members are all stakeholders in schools.

6. D: Choice *A* is incorrect because there is no way for teachers to ensure that caregivers actually completed the assignment with their student at home. While Choice *B* is a good suggestion, it is not the best option because once again, there is no way to ensure that caregivers are actually increasing their involvement at home. While teachers can certainly recommend resources, loaning them out from the classroom will result in lost materials, so Choice *C* is incorrect. Choice *D* is correct because it offers opportunities for caregivers to be directly involved in the classroom.

7. B: Flexibility is a central component of learner-centered education. Choice *A* is untrue because older materials may rely on outdated research. Choice *C* is false because combining two programs may allow teachers to benefit from the strengths of both methods. While talking to other teachers is a great idea, Choice *D* is not correct because your coworkers are not necessarily using the best programs in their classes.

8. C: Jasmine needs to assess the students first so that she knows which areas of the program need improvement. She can then modify the program, test her modifications, and reassess her students to see whether these modifications have been successful. Choice *A* cannot be true because modifying the program before identifying its weaknesses would be pointless. Choice *B* has the same problem, and it

Answer Explanations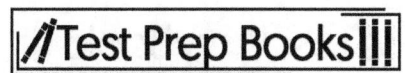

adds the mistake of reassessing students before experimenting with different techniques. Finally, Choice D adds another mistake by placing experimentation before the initial assessment.

9. C: Paraprofessionals help teachers but do not hold ultimate responsibility in the classroom. Choice A is untrue because paraprofessionals should not be working without teacher supervision. Choice B also places far too much responsibility on the paraprofessional. Choice D focuses on work outside the classroom, which is typically relegated to tutors rather than teaching aides.

10. C: Asking a paraprofessional to plan lessons, teach a class, or write tests and quizzes would be inappropriate because it asks them to work without the teacher's supervision and take full responsibility for the class. Choice C is appropriate because it occurs under the teacher's supervision and does not place too much responsibility on the paraprofessional.

11. A: Assessments should be frequent and ongoing for all students, but especially for those with special needs. These assessments may be informal but should be given daily after direct instruction and modeling. While summative assessments are important, they should not be the first and only assessment during a unit of study; usually summative assessments come at the end of a unit. Weekly and monthly assessments are too infrequent for remediation, intervention, or identification of struggling areas.

12. B: Since diagnostic assessments focus on specific skills, they meet Laura's needs best. A screening assessment, Choice A, screens for at-risk students instead of providing a more detailed assessment. A progress monitoring assessment, Choice C, is administered several times a year to track student progress. Outcomes assessments, Choice D, typically occur at the end of the year and are used to assess final understanding rather than diagnose concerns.

Reading Development: Foundational Skills

1. D: During the Emergent Spelling stage, children can identify letters but not the corresponding sounds. The other choices are fictitious.

2. A: Reciprocal teaching involves predicting, summarizing, questioning, and clarifying. The other choices are fictitious.

3. B: KWL charts are effective methods of activating prior knowledge and taking advantage of students' curiosity. Students can create a KWL (*know/want to know/learned*) chart to prepare for any unit of instruction and to generate questions about a topic.

4. D: Flashback is a technique used to give more background information in a story. None of the other concepts are directly related to going back in time.

5. A: Graphic organizers are methods of integrating knowledge and ideas. A graphic organizer can be one of many different visual tools for connecting concepts to help students understand information.

6. B: Making inferences is a method of deriving meaning that is intended by the author but not explicitly stated in the text. A flashback is a scene set earlier than the main story. Style is a general term for the way something is done. Figurative language is text that is not to be taken literally.

7. C: Genre is a means of categorizing text by its structure and literary elements. Fiction and nonfiction are both genre categories. Plot is the sequence of events that makes a story happen.

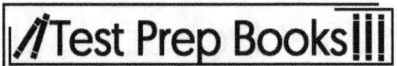

Answer Explanations

8. A: Scanning future portions of the text for information that helps resolve a question is an example of self-monitoring. Self-monitoring takes advantage of students' natural ability to recognize when they understand the reading and when they do not. KWL charts are used to help guide students to identify what they already know about a given topic. Metacognitive skills are when learners think about their thinking. Directed reading-thinking activities are done before and after reading to improve critical thinking and reading comprehension skills.

9. B: A reading corner is not designed to be a "hang out" for students, nor is it supposed to be a break location. Rather, it is a place for students to share thoughts on books or discuss recommendations. A reading corner should have books that are of appropriate reading level for students in the classroom.

10. A: Voice is the primary trait that shows the individual writing style of an author. It is based on an author's choice of common syntax, diction, punctuation, character development, dialogue, etc.

11. C: In order to check assessments for validity, it is important to understand what both question types entail for students. Selected-response questions cover a broad range of topics in a shorter period of time. However, students can guess the correct response on selected-response questions. Therefore, the results of select-response assessments are not always valid. Open-ended questions are longer and more time-consuming. However, these questions assess students' skill levels more effectively. Open-ended assessments also allow students to use text-based evidence to support their answers.

12. C: Ideas ultimately form the content of writing. The remaining choices are ways an author expresses their ideas.

13. A: The *sh* is an example of a consonant digraph, which is a combination of two consonants that work together to make a single sound. Examples of consonant digraphs are *sh*, *ch*, and *th*. Choice *B*, sound segmentation, is used to identify component phonemes in a word, such as separating the /t/, /u/, and /b/ in *tub*. Choice *C*, vowel digraph, is a set of two vowels that make up a single sound, such as *ow*, *ae*, or *ie*. Choice *D*, rime, is the sound that follows a word's onset, such as the /at/ in *cat*.

14. D: Phoneme segmentation is the identification of all the component phonemes in a word. An example would be the student identifying each separate sound, /t/, /u/, and /b/, in the word *tub*. Choice *A*, sound blending, is the blending together of two or more sounds in a word, such as /ch/ or /sh/. Choice *B*, substitution, occurs when a phoneme is substituted within a word for another phoneme, such as substituting the sound /b/ in *bun* to /r/ to create *run*. Choice *C*, rhyming, is an effective tool to utilize during the analytic phase of phonics development because rhyming words are often identical except for their beginning letters.

15. A: The alphabetic principle is the understanding that letters represent sounds in words. It is through the alphabetic principle that students learn the interrelationships between letter-sound (grapheme-phoneme) correspondences, phonemic awareness, and early decoding skills (such as sounding out and blending letter sounds).

16. D: Print awareness includes all of the answer choices except the spelling of sight words. Print awareness includes Choice *A*, the differentiation of uppercase and lowercase letters, so that students can understand which words begin a sentence. Choice *B*, the identification of word boundaries, is also included in print awareness; that is, students should be made aware that words are made up of letters and that spaces appear between words, etc. Choice *C*, the proper tracking of words, is also included in print awareness; this is the realization that print is organized in a particular way.

Answer Explanations

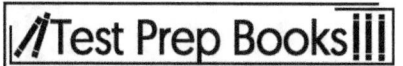

17. D: Option *I*, word boundaries, is one of the factors modeled because as teachers point to individual words, they indicate separation between the words. Directionality is the ability to track words as they are being read, so this is also modeled. One-to-one correspondence, the last factor listed, is the ability to match written letters to words to spoken words when reading. It is another thing teachers model when they point to words while they read.

18. B: Structural analysis focuses on the meaning of morphemes. Morphemes include base words, prefixes, and word endings (inflections and suffixes) that are found within longer words. Students can use structural analysis skill to find familiar word parts within an unfamiliar word in order to decode the word and determine the definition of the new word. The prefix *im-* (meaning not) in the word *improbable* can help students derive the definition of an event that is not likely to occur.

19. B: The student is performing at the phonetic stage. Phonetic spellers will spell a word as it sounds. The speller perceives and represents all of the phonemes in a word. However, because phonetic spellers have limited sight word vocabulary, irregular words are often spelled incorrectly.

20. B: The creation of word walls, Choice *I*, is advantageous during the phonetic stage of spelling development. On a word wall, words that share common consonant-vowel patterns or letter clusters are written in groups. Choices *II* and *III*, daily reading and writing opportunities, are also important in spelling instructions. Students need daily opportunities in order to review and practice spelling development. A spelling inventory, Choice *IV*, is different than a traditional spelling test because students are not allowed to study the words prior to the administration of a spelling inventory. Therefore, this option is incorrect as it mentions the inventory contains words students have studied all week.

21. A: The teacher should have the student use a think-aloud to verbalize the directions of the shapes used when writing each letter. During think-alouds, teachers voice the metacognitive process that occurs when writing each part of a given letter. Students should be encouraged to do likewise when practicing writing the letters.

22. D: Teachers should capitalize on the transfer of relevant skills from the learner's original language(s). In this way, extra attention and instructional emphasis can be applied toward the teaching of sounds and meanings of words that are nontransferable between the two languages.

23. C: Writing samples are the most appropriate assessment of spelling for students who are performing at the pre-phonetic stage. During the pre-phonetic stage, students participate in pre-communicative writing, which appears to be a jumble of letter-like forms rather than a series of discrete letters. Samples of students' pre-communicative writing can be used to assess their understanding of the alphabetic principle and their knowledge of letter-sound correspondences.

24. A: Phonological awareness is best assessed through identification of rimes or onsets within words. Instruction of phonological awareness includes detecting and identifying word boundaries, syllables, onsets/rimes, and rhyming words.

25. A: The identification of morphemes within words occurs during the instruction of structural analysis. Structural analysis is a word recognition skill that focuses on the meanings of word parts, or morphemes, during the introduction of a new word. Choice *B*, syllabic analysis, is a word analysis skill that helps students split words into syllables. Choice *C*, phonics, is the direct correspondence between

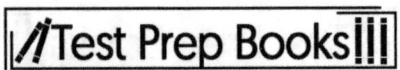

Answer Explanations

and blending of letters and sounds. Choice *D*, the alphabetic principle, teaches that letters or other characters represent sounds.

26. B: Homophones are words that are pronounced the same way but differ in meaning and/or spelling. *To* and *too* are homophones because they are pronounced the same way but differ in both meaning and spelling. Choices *A*, *C*, and *D* are not homophones because they do not sound the same when spoken aloud.

27. B: Nursery rhymes are used in kindergarten to develop phoneme recognition. Rhyming words are often almost identical except for their beginning letter(s), so rhyming is a great strategy to implement during the analytic phase of phoneme development.

28. B: High-frequency words are taught during the instruction of sight word recognition. Sight words, sometimes referred to as high-frequency words, are words that are used often but may not follow the regular principles of phonics. Sight words may also be defined as words that students are able to recognize and read without having to sound out.

29. C: Decoding should be assessed in context and in isolation. To assess in context, students read passages from appropriate texts aloud to the teacher so that the teacher can analyze their approach to figuring out unknown words. Decoding should also be assessed in isolation. In these types of assessments, students are given a list of words and/or phonics patterns. Initially, high-frequency words that follow predictable phonics patterns are presented. The words that are presented become more challenging as a student masters less difficult words.

30. D: Repeated readings is most likely NOT a reason for the difficulty the student is experiencing. Poor word recognition, a lack of content vocabulary, and inadequate background knowledge can all affect someone's sight vocabulary.

31. A: There is a positive correlation between a student's exposure to text and the academic achievement of that individual. Therefore, students should be given ample opportunities to read as much text as possible independently in order to gain vocabulary and background knowledge.

32. C: By definition, morphology is the identification and use of morphemes such as root words and affixes. Listening comprehension refers to the processes involved in understanding spoken language. Word consciousness refers to the knowledge required for students to learn and effectively utilize language. Textual analysis is an approach that researchers use to gain information and describe the characteristics of a recorded or visual message.

33. C: The five basic components of reading education are phonemic awareness, phonics, fluency, vocabulary, and comprehension.

34. A: If a child can accurately read text with consistent speed and appropriate expression while demonstrating comprehension, the child is said to have reading fluency skills. Without the ability to read fluently, a child's reading comprehension, Choice *C*, will be limited.

35. B: Phonics is the ability to apply letter-sound relationships and letter patterns in order to pronounce written words accurately. Phonemic awareness is the understanding that words are comprised of a combination of sounds. Fluency is an automatic recognition and accurate interpretation of text. Vocabulary is the body of words that a person knows.

Answer Explanations

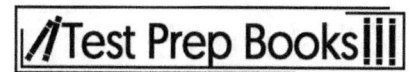

36. C: Comprehension is the level of content understanding that a student demonstrates after reading. Orthographic development is a cumulative process for learning to read, with each skill building on the previously mastered skill. Fluency is an automatic recognition and accurate interpretation of text. Phonics is the ability to apply letter-sound relationships and letter patterns in order to accurately pronounce written words.

37. C: A phoneme is the smallest unit of sound (for example, the phonogram "ph" represents the phoneme /f/). Choice A, a word, is typically composed of multiple phonemes. Choice B refers to phonics, and Choice D is a subtype of phoneme.

38. B: Pragmatics is the study of what words mean in certain situations. Choice A, morphology, involves the structure and formation of words. Choice C, syntax, refers to the order of words in a sentence. Choice D, semantics, addresses the distinct meanings of words.

Reading Development: Comprehension

1. D: Students who bring extensive background knowledge to the classroom are likely to experience easier automation when reading. In this way, background knowledge and reading comprehension are directly related. Likewise, students who have greater background knowledge are able to learn a greater number of new concepts at a faster rate.

2. D: Practice is an essential component of effective fluency instruction. A student's accuracy and rate will likely increase if a teacher provides for them opportunities to learn words and use word-analysis skills.

3. B: DRTA incorporates both read-alouds and think-alouds. During a DRTA, students make predictions about the text at hand in order to set a purpose for reading, give cognitive focus, and activate prior knowledge. Students use reading comprehension in order to verify their predictions.

4. C: A student's reading ability will most likely differ when assessed via a reading assessment versus a writing sample. There are five types of vocabulary: listening, speaking, written, sight, and meaning. Most often, listening vocabulary contains the greatest number of words. This is usually followed by speaking vocabulary, sight reading vocabulary, meaning vocabulary, and written vocabulary. Formal written language usually utilizes a richer vocabulary than everyday oral language. Thus, students show differing strengths in reading vocabulary and writing vocabulary.

5. B: Scaffolded opportunities occur when a teacher helps students by giving them support, offering immediate feedback, and suggesting strategies. In order to be beneficial, such feedback needs to help students identify areas that need improvement. Much like oral reading feedback, this advice increases students' awareness so they can independently make needed modifications in order to improve fluency. Scaffolding is lessened as the student becomes a more independent reader. Scaffolding is lessened as the student becomes a more independent reader. Students with diverse learning profiles benefit from direct instruction and feedback that teaches decoding and analysis of unknown words, automaticity in key sight words, and correct expression and phrasing.

6. B: Key indicators of reading fluency include accuracy, rate, and prosody. Phonetics and decodable skills aid fluency. Syntax, semantics, word morphology, listening comprehension, and word exposure aid vocabulary development.

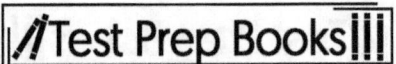

Answer Explanations

7. A: Once students become fluent readers, independent reading can begin. Students who do not yet display automaticity may need to read out loud or whisper to themselves during independent reading time. Independent silent reading accompanied by comprehension accountability is an appropriate strategy for students who demonstrate automaticity in their decoding skills. Also, each student should be provided with a text that matches their reading level.

8. C: The most common measurement of reading rate includes the oral contextual timed readings of students. During a timed reading, the number of errors made within a given amount of time is recorded. This data can be used to identify if a student's rate is improving and if the rate falls within the recommended range for his or her grade level.

9. A: Syntax refers to the arrangement of words and phrases to form well-developed sentences and paragraphs. Semantics has to do with language meaning. Grammar is a composite of all systems and structures utilized within a language and includes syntax, word morphology, semantics, and phonology. Cohesion and coherence of oral and written language are promoted through a full understanding of syntax, semantics, and grammar.

10. B: Informal reading assessments allow teachers to create differentiated assessments that target reading skills of individual students. In this way, teachers can gain insight into a student's reading strengths and weaknesses. Informal assessments can help teachers decide what content and strategies need to be targeted. However, standardized reading assessments provide all students with the same structure to assess multiple skills at one time. Standardized reading assessments cannot be individualized. Such assessments are best used for gaining an overview of student reading abilities.

11. D: Students within a single classroom come with varied background knowledge, interests, and needs. Thus, it is unrealistic to find texts that apply to all. Students benefit when a wide range of fiction and nonfiction texts are available in a variety of genres, promoting differentiated instruction.

12. D: This answer alludes to both read-alouds and think-alouds. Modeling fluency can be done through read-alouds. Proper pace, phrasing, and expression of text can be modeled when teachers read aloud to their students. During think-alouds, teachers verbalize their thought processes when orally reading a selection. Teachers' explanations may describe strategies they use as they read to monitor their comprehension. In this way, teachers explicitly model the metacognition processes that good readers use to construct meaning from a text.

13. A: Reading fluency is the ability to accurately read at a socially acceptable pace and with proper expression. Phonetic awareness leads to the proper pronunciation of words and fluency. Once students are able to read fluently, concentration is no longer dedicated toward the process of reading. Instead, students can concentrate on the meaning of a text. Thus, in the developmental process of reading, comprehension follows fluency.

14. A: The rhythmic sounds and rhyming words of some poems help build a child's phonemic awareness.

15. D: The teacher records how many words each student reads correctly when reading aloud a list of a teacher-selected, grade-appropriate words. Accuracy is measured as the percentage of words that are read correctly within a given text. Word-reading accuracy is often measured by counting the number of errors that occur per 100 words of oral reading. This information is used to select the appropriate level of text for an individual.

Answer Explanations

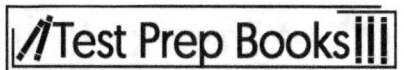

16. B: Nonfiction texts include memoirs, biographies, autobiographies, and journalism. Choices *A, C,* and *D* are all examples of fictional prose.

17. A: Summative assessments are formal assessments that are given at the end of a unit of study. These assessments are usually longer in length. They are not completed daily. These summative assessments should not be confused with informal assessments, which are used more frequently to determine mastery of the day's objective. However, summative assessments may be used to determine students' mastery in order to form intervention groups thereafter.

18. D: Boldfaced, highlighted, or italicized text notifies a student when a new vocabulary word or idea is present. Subtitles and headings can also alert a student to a change in topic or idea. These features are also important when answering questions, as a student may be able to find the answer easily with these typographic features present.

19. A: English Language Learners should master vocabulary and word usages in order to fully comprehend text. Figurative language, an author's purpose, and settings are more complex areas and are difficult for English Language Learners. These areas can be addressed once ELL students understand the meanings of words.

20. C: Choice *C* is an indication of a reliable source. Good research has high-quality content, is published by a reputable organization, and is written from an unbiased perspective. Choice *A* is incorrect; although many reliable sources are written by scholars, some sources written by scholars may be biased or not peer-reviewed. Choice *B* is incorrect because many internet sources are not reliable. Choice *D* is incorrect because older research often contains information that has been disproven by more recent research, so it is not necessarily reliable.

21. C: Freytag's pyramid maps the events that contribute to the general structure of a story's plot. Choices *A* and *B* involve course planning, and Choice *D* describes characters, which are not part of Freytag's pyramid.

22. C: Statement *I* is necessary for the book to truly bring a culture into your classroom. Statement *II* helps students engage with real-world problems and imitate positive behavior. Statement *IV* helps minority students feel included and educates students about their community. However, statement *III* is untrue because students can certainly learn about more than one culture at a time—in fact, comparing different cultures can help students analyze what they are learning.

Analysis and Response

1. C: Story maps are visual representations of story structures. They are a type of graphic organizer. Choice *A* is incorrect because the point is to work with the students and teach them how to organize the information rather than expecting them to learn from an online resource. Choice *B* is incorrect because letter tiles are used to teach younger children how to spell and break down individual words. Choice *D* is incorrect because word searches do not structurally organize elements of a story; they are puzzles where students search for a list of words in a grid.

2. B: Diagnostic reading assessments test students' word knowledge and phonemic awareness, including knowledge of syllables and sounds. Choice *A* is incorrect because pop quizzes are usually administered regularly to test children's knowledge of ongoing class instruction. Choice *C* is incorrect because norm-referenced assessments compare how children perform tasks in relation to others in their grade or age

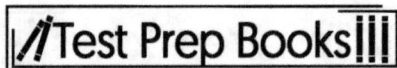

Answer Explanations

range. Choice *D* is incorrect because recitation is mostly used to see how well students remember the reading material they have been taught in class and if they are pronouncing words correctly.

3. A: Morphemes are important parts of words that cannot be broken down. Choice *B* is incorrect; prosody refers to the intonation patterns in syllables. Choice *C* is incorrect; semantics refers to the meaning of words, sentences, and other texts. Choice *D* is incorrect; inflectional suffixes are the grammatical ends of words.

4. D: Fables teach a moral or lesson, and they usually involve talking animals facing dilemmas. Choice *A* is incorrect; tall tales include details that are so exaggerated, they could not possibly be true. Choice *B* is incorrect; fairy tales often involve mythical creatures or supernatural elements and involve human beings as main characters rather than animals. Choice *C* is incorrect because legends are stories that usually involve some sort of historical element that cannot be proven true.

5. C: Beginners usually know the alphabet and about 600 words. At this stage, they should be taught to speak words phonetically and how to decode. Choice *A* is incorrect. Intermediate readers are usually in grades 3 through 10, they are able to decode, and reading will be a regular part of their lives. Choice *B* is incorrect; emergent readers are in the pre-alphabetic stage. They are usually between the ages of 6 months and 6 years and are becoming familiar with the look and feel of books. Choice *D* is incorrect; children in the transitional reading stage tend to be fluent readers learning the basics of grammar.

6. C: Delivering consistent, adequate material is a facet of reliability. Choice *A* is incorrect; assessing students' knowledge on the same scale describes equity. Choice *B* is incorrect; valid assessments are proven to be reputable and thoroughly cover the topics at hand. Choice *D* does not describe one of the three assessment concepts.

7. A: Norm-referenced tests compare national averages for children in the same age groups. Choices *B* and *C* are incorrect, and both describe criterion-referenced tests. These tests compare results to proposed standards of what children should learn by a certain grade, and they are usually ranked as below basic, basic, proficient, or advanced. Choice *D* is incorrect; children's knowledge is not compared to others' in different grades in norm-referenced tests.

8. B: The alphabetic principle teaches the relationships between letters and sounds. Choice *A* is incorrect because print concepts teach children to recognize text formatting, punctuation, and the direction text should be read in, among other things. Choice *C* is incorrect; semantics focuses on the meanings of words. Choice *D* is incorrect; morphemic awareness teaches children to recognize the morphemes, or roots, of different words.

9. D: Kinesthetic learners prefer an immersive, hands-on approach to learning. Choice *A* is incorrect; it describes visual learners, who respond best to the use of images. Choice *B* is incorrect as it describes auditory learners, who learn by listening. Choice *C* is incorrect because it is describing reading/writing learners, who learn best via the written word.

10. D: Children's patterned books are full of images that depict the words on the page and often use repetition and rhyming to help children remember the text. Choice *A* is incorrect; it is describing an autobiography, which provides a nonfiction account of a person's life. Choice *B* is incorrect as it is describing fairy tales, which are full of imaginary characters and settings. Choice *C* is incorrect because it is describing informational texts, which are factual and meant to educate.

Answer Explanations

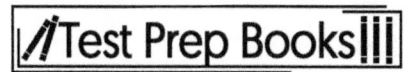

11. C: Homographs are spelled the same but have different meanings and sounds. Choice *A* is incorrect because contractions are formed when letters are left out of words to create shorter versions. Choice *B* is incorrect because homophones are words that sound alike but are different in meaning and spelling. Choice *D* is incorrect; determiners are words that introduce nouns.

12. A: Morphemic analysis involves studying the parts of words (roots, suffixes, etc.) and determining their meanings. Choice *B* is incorrect; breaking words down into syllables is syllabication. Choice *C* is incorrect because it is describing decoding, which is the assessment of letter-sound relationships. Choice *D* is incorrect; recognizing the patterns in words is basic word study.

13. B: Inflectional morphemes, such as *-ing*, *-est*, and *-'s*, make grammatical changes to words. Choice *A* is incorrect because those morphemes are contracted forms; contractions shorten words by removing certain letters but do not alter their definitions. Choice *C* is incorrect; these are examples of bound bases, which require prefixes or suffixes in order to make words. Choice *D* is incorrect because these morphemes are derivational; they are used to create new words or new versions of those words.

14. D: A copula is a word that connects the subject of a sentence to a complement. Choices *A*, *B*, and *C* are incorrect because they are all examples of uncommon vowels. A schwa is a syllable that does not make a short or long vowel sound. A consonant-le occurs when a consonant is followed by -le. An open vowel is formed when the tongue is not near the roof of the mouth (*a, e, i, o, u*).

15. D: Identifying vowels and syllable division patterns is generally how to teach syllabication. Choices *A*, *B*, and *C* are incorrect. Reciting the text repeatedly may help with pronunciation of syllables, but it will not show students how to break words down. Pairing students off and administering frequent spelling tests will not necessarily teach students syllabication but will help with reading fluency and vocabulary knowledge.

16. B: PALS stands for Peer-Assisted Learning Strategies.

17. A: The three levels of reading comprehension are literal, inferential, and evaluative.

18. C: Carey is using graphic organizers. Choice *A* is incorrect. Although slideshows can include images and other diagrams, the question does not mention the defining feature of slideshows, which is the sliding format. Choice *B* is incorrect. Word tiles are usually virtual or physical blocks that teachers use to teach spelling and syllabication. Choice *D* is incorrect; a patterned book uses rhyming words and repetition to help children memorize stories.

Dear TExES Science of Teaching Reading Test Taker,

Thank you for purchasing this study guide for your TExES Science of Teaching Reading exam. We hope that we exceeded your expectations.

Our goal in creating this study guide was to cover all of the topics that you will see on the test. We also strove to make our practice questions as similar as possible to what you will encounter on test day. With that being said, if you found something that you feel was not up to your standards, please send us an email and let us know.

We would also like to let you know about other books in our catalog that may interest you.

TExES Core Subjects EC-6

This can be found on Amazon: amazon.com/dp/1637755147

TExES English Language Arts and Reading 7-12

amazon.com/dp/1637750366

TExES Math 7-12

amazon.com/dp/163775874X

TExES Social Studies 7-12

amazon.com/dp/1637751184

We have study guides in a wide variety of fields. If the one you are looking for isn't listed above, then try searching for it on Amazon or send us an email.

Thanks Again and Happy Testing!
Product Development Team
support@testprepbooks.com

Online Resources & Audiobook

Included with your purchase are multiple online resources. This includes the practice tests in an interactive format and this book in audiobook format.

Scan the QR code or go to this link to access this content:

testprepbooks.com/online387/texes-sci-teach-read

The first time you access the page, you will need to register as a "new user" and verify your email address.

If you have any issues, please email support@testprepbooks.com.

Thank you for letting us be a part of your studying journey!